TULAREMIA

Anthrax

Avian Flu

Botulism

Campylobacteriosis

Cholera

Ebola

Encephalitis

Escherichia coli Infections

Gonorrhea

Hantavirus Pulmonary Syndrome

Hepatitis

Herpes

HIV/AIDS

Infectious Fungi

Influenza

Legionnaires' Disease

Leprosy

Lyme Disease

Mad Cow Disease (Bovine Spongiform Encephalopathy)

Malaria

Meningitis

Mononucleosis

Pelvic Inflammatory Disease

Plague

Polio

Salmonella

SARS

Smallpox

Streptococcus (Group A)

Staphylococcus aureus Infections

Syphilis

Toxic Shock Syndrome

Tuberculosis

Tularemia

Typhoid Fever

West Nile Virus

DEADLY DISEASES AND EPIDEMICS

TULAREMIA

Susan Hutton Siderovski

FOUNDING EDITOR
The Late **I. Edward Alcamo**
Distinguished Teaching Professor of Microbiology,
SUNY Farmingdale

FOREWORD BY
David Heymann
World Health Organization

CHELSEA HOUSE
P U B L I S H E R S
An imprint of Infobase Publishing

Tularemia

Copyright © 2006 by Infobase Publishing

Chelsea House
An imprint of Infobase Publishing
132 West 31st Street
New York NY 10001

Library of Congress Cataloging-in-Publication Data

Siderovski, Susan Hutton, 1964–
  Tularemia/Susan Hutton Siderovski.
    p. cm. — (Deadly diseases and epidemics)
  ISBN 0-7910-8679-8
  1. Tularemia—Juvenile literature. I. Title. II. Series.
RA421.S52 2005
614.5'739—dc22   2005021239

Text design by Terry Mallon
Cover design by Keith Trego

Printed in the United States of America

Bang 21C 10 9 8 7 6 5 4 3 2 1

This book is printed on acid-free paper.

Table of Contents

Foreword

In the 1960s, many of the infectious diseases that had terrorized generations were tamed. After a century of advances, the leading killers of Americans both young and old were being prevented with new vaccines or cured with new medicines. The risk of death from pneumonia, tuberculosis (TB), meningitis, influenza, whooping cough, and diphtheria declined dramatically. New vaccines lifted the fear that summer would bring polio, and a global campaign was on the verge of eradicating smallpox worldwide. New pesticides like DDT cleared mosquitoes from homes and fields, thus reducing the incidence of malaria, which was present in the southern United States and which remains a leading killer of children worldwide. New technologies produced safe drinking water and removed the risk of cholera and other waterborne diseases. Science seemed unstoppable. Disease seemed destined to all but disappear.

But the euphoria of the 1960s has evaporated.

The microbes fought back. Those causing diseases like TB and malaria evolved resistance to cheap and effective drugs. The mosquito developed the ability to defuse pesticides. New diseases emerged, including AIDS, Legionnaires' disease, and Lyme disease. And diseases that had not been seen in decades re-emerged, as the hantavirus did in the Navajo Nation in 1993. Technology itself actually created new health risks. The global transportation network, for example, meant that diseases like West Nile virus could spread beyond isolated regions and quickly become global threats. Even modern public health protections sometimes failed, as they did in 1993 in Milwaukee, Wisconsin, resulting in 400,000 cases of the digestive system illness cryptosporidiosis. And, more recently, the threat from smallpox, a disease believed to be completely eradicated, has returned along with other potential bioterrorism weapons such as anthrax.

The lesson is that the fight against infectious diseases will never end.

In our constant struggle against disease, we as individuals have a weapon that does not require vaccines or drugs, and that is the warehouse of knowledge. We learn from the history of science that "modern" beliefs can be wrong. In this series of books, for example, you will learn that diseases like syphilis were once thought to be caused by eating potatoes. The invention of the microscope set science on the right path. There are more positive lessons from history. For example, smallpox was eliminated by vaccinating everyone who had come in contact with an infected person. This "ring" approach to smallpox control is still the preferred method for confronting an outbreak, should the disease be intentionally reintroduced.

At the same time, we are constantly adding new drugs, new vaccines, and new information to the warehouse. Recently, the entire human genome was decoded. So too was the genome of the parasite that causes malaria. Perhaps by looking at the microbe and the victim through the lens of genetics we will be able to discover new ways to fight malaria, which remains the leading killer of children in many countries.

Because of advances in our understanding of such diseases as AIDS, entire new classes of anti-retroviral drugs have been developed. But resistance to all these drugs has already been detected, so we know that AIDS drug development must continue.

Education, experimentation, and the discoveries that grow out of them are the best tools to protect health. Opening this book may put you on the path of discovery. I hope so, because new vaccines, new antibiotics, new technologies, and, most importantly, new scientists are needed now more than ever if we are to remain on the winning side of this struggle against microbes.

David Heymann
Executive Director
Communicable Diseases Section
World Health Organization
Geneva, Switzerland

1
Introduction

PET HAMSTER SCARE

Three-year-old Matt and his parents in Denver, Colorado, bought six hamsters in January 2004 from the local pet store, but each hamster died from diarrhea within the first week home. Matt also fell ill. At first, no one made the connection between the little bite on Matt's arm and his high fever and the swollen lymph node in his armpit. His parents took him to the family doctor for treatment, but the usual course of antibiotic failed to improve his intermittent fevers. The lymph node in his armpit became quite big, swollen, and very tender. Forty-nine days from the onset of Matt's sickness, a decision was made to take a tissue sample of his swollen lymph node to try and identify his infection in order to better focus his treatment and stop the infection.

The Colorado Department of Public Health and Environment (CDPHE) inspected the pet store. Workers at the store confirmed an unusual number of hamster deaths in January 2004. From lists obtained from the pet store of hamster purchases from December to February, 15 of 18 customers were located and interviewed. Eight hamsters in the Denver metropolitan area homes had died within two weeks of the date of purchase. The breeders and suppliers who provided the hamsters to the pet store were interviewed but reported no unusual deaths in their hamster populations (Figure 1.1).

Matt's tissue sample was cultured. The results suggested that it was likely that he was infected with *Francisella tularensis,* a type of bacteria that causes an infection called tularemia. At the CDPHE laboratory, **polymerase chain reaction (PCR)** testing of **deoxyribonucleic acid (DNA)** from the tissue sample confirmed the diagnosis as

Figure 1.1 Household pets can easily contract infectious diseases in pet stores and transmit the bacteria to their new family.

tularemia. The site of Matt's hamster bite was raised and the skin was peeling off Matt's arm—this was the most probable site of entry of the *F. tularensis* bacteria causing Matt's tularemia.

Pet store workers reported that there were two store cats that were free to roam around the store. Blood taken from one of the cats was positive for *F. tularensis*. Previously, a similar **outbreak** had occurred at a local zoo, leading the health investigators to speculate that wild rodents infected with *F. tularensis* could be to blame for the spread of the infection to the pet store.[1] The cat that tested positive for *F. tularensis*

(continued on page 12)

THE AGENT-HOST-ENVIRONMENT MODEL

The agent-host-environment model is used by researchers who investigate **epidemiologic** outbreaks (**epidemiologists**) to understand how interrelated factors affect the transmission of infectious diseases. The model has three components that are central to understanding how disease propagates (See figure).

The first component is the agent. In the case of microbial diseases, the agent is a bacterium, virus, parasite, or fungus. Factors that can control the infectious potential of an agent include its virulence, concentration, **resistance** to treatment, ability to produce toxin, and ability to survive outside the host. Any of these factors can influence the potential for an agent to multiply and harm the human host.

The **host** is the person impacted by the agent—the person who has a chance of becoming infected. The health status of the person is a significant determinant of his or her chance of becoming infected. Age, immune status (whether the person has been immunized or, alternatively, if he or she is immuno-compromised), genetics, pre-existing health conditions, edu-cation, and fitness level are factors that affect health. For workers in a specific occupation, their knowledge and adher-ence to personal protective procedures are additional signifi-cant factors that contribute to their risk of exposure to the infectious agent. These host factors determine the magnitude to which the agent impacts the health of the host population.

The environment represents the conditions outside the host that allow for the possibility of disease transmission. Population density (especially for agents that transmit from person to person), **vectors** (*e.g.*, insects or inanimate objects), **reservoirs**, temperature, and societal environment (*e.g.*, access to health care providers), when favorable to the agent, will advance the spread of infection. Targeting infec-tious diseases using the agent-host-environment model, and

intercepting their spread with such measures as immunization, sanitation, pest control, and nutritional improvements,
can lead to a decline in **morbidity** and **mortality** in the
host population.

Source: Timmreck, Thomas C. *An Introduction to Epidemiology*. Boston,
MA: Jones and Bartlett Publishers, 1994.

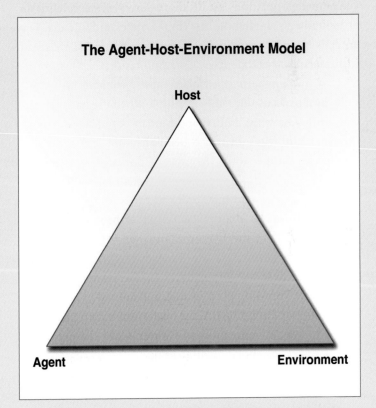

The triangle of epidemiology is used to analyze the roles and
inter-relationships between host, agent, and environment in the
spreading of disease. A change in any one of these variables
either increases or decreases the frequency of the disease.

(continued from page 9)

must have gotten the infection by catching and eating an infected wild rodent. The store owner was advised to set traps for wild rodents and to inform the state health department of any recurrent animal deaths or reports of ill customers or staff.

THE SPREAD OF TULAREMIA IN NATURE

Some 100 animal species can carry *F. tularensis* infection. The continual presence of *F. tularensis* bacteria in North American animal populations means that tularemia in animals is an **enzoonotic** disease in both the United States and Canada. The animals most commonly associated with tularemia are small mammals, such as rodents, rabbits, and muskrats. Most countries in the northern hemisphere have problems with sporadic outbreaks of tularemia in people when the bacterium is transmitted between animal and human populations. Unlike influenza outbreaks, in which people readily spread the disease to one another when they sneeze, humans are accidental hosts of *F. tularensis* and person-to-person spread is not a concern.

In addition to mammals, biting **arthropods** such as deerflies, ticks (in the United States), and mosquitoes (in Scandinavian countries) are known vectors that spread tularemia. These are key sources in the **transmission** of *F. tularensis* from animal to animal, and animal to man. Also, in the outdoor environment, the bacterium has an incredible ability to stay alive in mud and water. Cold temperatures do not easily destabilize the bacterium. Even infected rabbit carcasses that were frozen for three years have caused tularemia when the meat was used in a rabbit stew cooked at too low a temperature to kill the bacteria. Scandinavian farmers working in their fields have developed pneumonic tularemia from simply disturbing hay that was infected with *F. tularensis* (due to infected vole droppings). Outbreaks of tularemia in landscapers due to **aerosolized**

F. tularensis from animal sources occurred in Martha's Vineyard, Massachusetts in 1978 and 2000.

RABBIT SEASON?

The longstanding association of rabbits with tularemia in hunters gave the disease the nickname of "rabbit fever." Tularemia is the name one bacteriologist gave the infection after realizing its source was a single agent. Different facets and manifestations of the disease, depending on how the disease was transmitted, presented a paradox to bacteriologists and physicians at the turn of the 20th century (Table 1.1). Initially believed to be many different medical conditions, tularemia was discovered to arise from a single **infectious agent,** the bacterium *F. tularensis.*

Matt's case of tularemia highlights the continued presence of *F. tularensis* in the United States to this day. **Isolated cases** of tularemia continue to occur in veterinarians exposed to *F. tularensis* following treatment of domestic cats. Laboratory workers can contract *F. tularensis* during blood sample analysis or tularemia vaccine research. Tularemia is the third most common **laboratory-acquired** infectious disease after brucellosis and typhoid fever. The **virulence** and prolonged course of symptoms by which *F. tularensis* disables people were of particular interest to military strategists who for many decades sought to research, refine, modify, weaponize, and stockpile this bacterium as a biological weapon. *F. tularensis* has an extensive history summarized in Table 1.2.

With fewer than 200 cases per year in the United States, tularemia may not seem a significant health hazard. However, history tells the true picture of the nature and potential of the bacterium to affect the health of people across the globe. *F. tularensis* has played a role in military history as a biological weapon and remains a potential threat for widespread harm to human health in the future.

Table 1.1 Manifestations of Tularemia at the Turn of the 20th Century

Name of Condition	Researcher, Year
Conjunctivitis tularensis	Martin, 1907 and Fred W. Lamb, 1917
Plague-like disease of rodents in California	McCoy, 1911
Deer-fly fever in Utah	Pearse, 1911 Francis and Mayne, 1920
Rabbit fever	Vail, B. H. Lamb and Wherry, 1914
Market men's disease in Washington, D.C.	Thompson, 1921
Typhoidal type of tularemia in lab workers	Lake and Francis, 1921
Glandular form of tick fever in Montana and Idaho	Lamb of Idaho, 1923
Ohara's disease in Japan	Ohara, 1925
Water-rat trappers disease in Obdorsk, Russia	Zarhi, 1929

Source: Jellison, W. L. "Tularemia." *Bulletin History of Medicine* 96(1972): 477–485 (p. 484).

Table 1.2 Timeline of Significant Events in the History of Tularemia.

Date	Events
1932–1945	Japan Unit 731 infects Chinese citizens and prisoners of war with *F. tularensis.*
1942	Battle of Stalingrad in the Second World War involves Russian use of *F. tularensis* against German troops.
1954–1973	The U.S. military researches the effect of tularemia on human volunteers in inhalation experiments.
1966	Largest outbreak of airborne tularemia causes over 600 cases in north-central Sweden.
1971–1973	U.S. destroys weaponized *F. tularensis* stockpiles.
1978	Martha's Vineyard, Massachusetts experiences an outbreak of inhaled *F. tularensis.*
1979	The Soviet Biopreparat continues its research of *F. tularensis* and develops an antibiotic-resistant strain.
1982	Soviet researchers drop bombs filled with vaccine-resistant *F. tularensis* onto 500 immunized monkeys on Rebirth Island.
1997	Spain reports 585 tularemia cases attributed to hare hunting.
2000	Martha's Vineyard has a second outbreak of inhaled tularemia related to lawn mowing.
2003	The U.S. National Institutes of Health funds research for early detection devices and tularemia vaccine development.
2004	U.S. state public health departments hold emergency preparedness drills using mock tularemia terrorism scenarios.

2

An Early History of the First American Disease

PLAGUE-LIKE DISEASE OF RODENTS

Beginning in 1885, 12 million deaths in China and India were attributed to bubonic plaque. It spread around the planet and arrived in San Francisco's Chinatown in 1900. In the following four years, there were 126 cases (with 122 deaths) in the greater San Francisco area. A devastating earthquake and fire in San Francisco in 1906 raised fears of an outbreak of plague among the survivors and occupants of refugee encampments. Not only were the people homeless, but there were now millions of rats running free. The fleas of the rats were spreading the bacteria that caused plague. In the year following the earthquake (1907), there were 160 cases (with 77 deaths) in San Francisco.

Dr. George Walter McCoy worked for the United States Public Health Service (USPHS) as a bacteriologist, immunologist, and epidemiologist from 1900 to 1940. As Director of the USPHS Plague Laboratory, Dr. McCoy was sent to San Francisco in 1907 to investigate reports of bubonic plague outbreaks. At the same time that McCoy was investigating the plague, Dr. William Buchanan Wherry arrived at the Oakland Medical School to work both as an M.D. and a bacteriologist for the San Francisco Board of Health. Wherry was in touch with his friend and colleague George McCoy, both of whom had worked for the government medical service stationed in Manila, Philippine Islands, at the turn of the century.

Rats infected with plague wandered into rural forest areas beyond San Francisco. The fleas were spreading to wild rats, squirrels, and prairie dogs, permanently establishing plague in a transmission cycle between wild small mammals and fleas (defined as sylvatic plague). In Oakland in 1907, Wherry discovered sylvatic plague in California ground squirrels.

George McCoy's research led him to the outskirts of Fresno, California, some 210 miles from San Francisco. In Tulare County outside of Fresno in 1911, Dr. McCoy observed squirrels dying of a disease that caused plague-like sores. McCoy knew he had found an illness that was different from plague. He dubbed the new animal disease a plague-like disease of rodents.

In 1911, Drs. McCoy and Charles C. Chapin isolated the **pathogen** responsible for the new disease. The organism was difficult to **culture** in ordinary growth broths, but was finally isolated from a newly developed coagulated egg yolk culture medium that the researchers had perfected. The work was published in 1912 and the new organism was named after the county in which plague-like disease of rodents was first found: Tulare County, California. The bacterium was then known as *Bacillus tularense*.

Even after his move to the University of Cincinnati in 1909, Dr. Wherry kept up communication with Dr. McCoy. In 1913, assisted by B. H. Lamb, Wherry recognized an eye infection in a restaurant worker as being identical to the disease recently published by McCoy and Chapin. This would be the first bacteriologically confirmed case of *Bacillus tularense* infection in man. Wherry and Lamb published their findings in 1914, in an article entitled "A new bacterial disease of rodents transmissible to man."[1]

DEER-FLY FEVER

The USPHS sent Dr. Edward Francis, a surgeon and bacteriologist, to investigate deer-fly fever cases in Utah. Between 1917 and 1920 in Millard County, Utah, there had been two dozen human cases of a new disease that caused high fever following deerfly bites (Figure 2.1). Immediately after the bite, patients

(continued on page 22)

THE AGGLUTINATION TEST

An agglutination reaction was used by McCoy and Chapin in 1911 to test for infection with *Bacillus tularense* (See figure). Samples of the bacteria from naturally infected ground squirrels were grown on coagulated egg yolk at 37°C for two days. Guinea pigs were injected with the bacteria and blood serum was obtained one to two weeks later. Adding *B. tularense* bacteria directly to the blood serum of infected guinea pigs gave a cloudy appearance, but the blood serum of uninfected control guinea pigs remained clear. The cloudy appearance is the result of agglutination. The agglutination (or clumping) of bacteria indicates a previous exposure of the host to *F. tularensis* infection. These antibodies are bivalent, having two identical binding sites for specific antigens (proteins, sugars, or lipids) on the surface of the *B. tularense* bacterium. These antibodies are not present in the blood serum of animals or humans that have not been exposed to *B. tularense*.

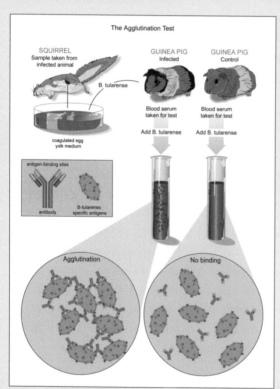

The Agglutination Test

SQUIRREL
Sample taken from infected animal

B. tularense

coagulated egg yolk medium

antigen-binding sites

antibody   B-tularense specific antigens

GUINEA PIG
Infected

GUINEA PIG
Control

Blood serum taken for test   Blood serum taken for test

Add B. tularense   Add B. tularense

Agglutination   No binding

In the **agglutination test,** *Bacillus tularense* from squirrels was cultured and injected into guinea pigs. Later, adding the bacteria to the guinea pig serum produces clumping or agglutination in infected guinea pigs. The agglutination indicates previous exposure to the bacteria.

Figure 2.1 In Utah between 1917 and 1920, deerflies were the cause of multiple cases of tularemia in humans until Dr. Edward Francis made the connection following the first death from "Deer-Fly Fever."

Table 2.1 History of Tularemia

TULAREMIA: THE FIRST AMERICAN DISEASE

The physicians of this country should be thrilled by the thought that our knowledge of this disease has been entirely developed by American workers.

(Simpson, 1929)

Date	Event
1907	Dr. Ancil Martin, an ophthalmologist and president of the Arizona Medical Association in 1894, writes of five novel human cases of eye infection in his practice.
1911	Dr. George Walter McCoy investigates the plague and discovers a new plague-like disease of rodents in Tulare County, California.
1911	Dr. R. A. Pearse of Utah describes six human cases of deer-fly fever.
1912	Drs. McCoy and Charles C. Chapin, studying plague-like disease of rodents, isolate the causative organism on coagulated egg yolk medium. They name the bacterium *Bacillus tularense* after Tulare County.
1914	Drs. William Buchanan Wherry, a professor at the University of Cincinnati, and B. H. Lamb publish the first report of a bacteriologically confirmed case of human infection with *B. tularense* in the *Journal of Infectious Disease*. Drs. D. T. Vail, B. H. Lamb, and Wherry also isolate *B. tularense* from a dead cottontail rabbit.
1917	Dr. Frederick W. Lamb publishes a report entitled "Conjunctivitis tularensis" in the *Ophthalmology Record*.

1919	Dr. Edward Francis, a surgeon with the USPHS, reports the first fatal human case related to a Millard County, Utah outbreak of two dozen cases of deer-fly fever from 1917–1920.
1921	Dr. Francis concludes that plague-like disease of rodents and deer-fly fever were both caused by *B. tularense* and that *B. tularense* disease in man should be named "tularemia."
1922	Dr. G. C. Lake, assistant surgeon, and Dr. Edward Francis report six cases of tularemia in USPHS laboratory workers over two years, highlighting the increased occupational safety risk associated with work on *B. tularense* in the laboratory.
1924	Dr. R. R. Parker, special expert, USPHS in Hamilton, Montana, and Dr. R. R. Spencer, Director of the Hygienic Laboratory in Washington, D.C., identify the role of the wood tick in the transmission of tularemia. Dr. Parker isolates *B. tularense* from a guinea pig exposed to infected ticks. Five years later, they would show that ticks pass the bacterium to their eggs, establishing ticks as a reservoir of tularemia.
1928	Dr. Francis summarizes the clinical and epidemiologic features of tularemia with his experience confirming more than 800 cases. He also confirms that samples from Dr. Ohara in Japan of three patients exposed during the skinning of a rabbit contain *B. tularense*. This discovery establishes the broader distribution of tularemia beyond the United States.
1959	Dr. Francis is honored by Russian physicians N. G. Olsufjev, O.S. Emelyanova, and T. N. Dunayeva, who propose the name of *B. tularense* be changed to *Francisella tularensis*.

Sources:

Evans, M. E., D. W. Gregory, W. Schaffner, and Z. A. McGee. "Tularemia: A 30-Year Experience with 88 Cases." *Medicine* 64(4)(1985):251–269.

Simpson, Walter M. *Tularemia: History, Pathology, Diagnosis and Treatment.* New York, NY Paul B. Hoeber, 1929.

(continued from page 17)

felt the onset of pain and fever, and their lymph glands became swollen and tender and developed pus. The fever lasted three to six weeks and a slow **convalescence** followed. On September 12, 1919, the first fatal case in man was reported by Francis in an article in *Public Health Reports* entitled "Deer-Fly Fever: A Disease of Man of Hitherto Unknown **Etiology**."[2]

From the blood samples he had taken from deer-fly fever patients, Francis was able to isolate the cause of the disease. It was *B. tularense.* From 1919 to 1920, he identified seven bacteriologically confirmed cases of infection in humans and 17 infected jackrabbits in his laboratory in Washington, D.C. Dr. Francis, assisted by B. Mayne, made the connection between these Utah cases and McCoy's rodent disease (Figure 2.2). In the Utah cases, the deerfly *Chrysops discalis* served as a vector, transmitting the bacterium from rabbit to rabbit. Because the infection was found in human blood, Francis called the disorder "tularemia."

The disease was found to affect people in rural communities who worked in fields and were bitten by deerflies. In his 1921 report, Francis was quick to note the significant impact of the disease on the economy of the community:

> The chief interest in tularemia as a disease of man arises from the disability which accompanies the illness; a disabling illness which overtakes the farmer in the busy season of midsummer, causing two or three months of sickness in the harvest season, is a serious matter.[3]

On November 11, 1927, Dr. Francis gave a lecture to a New York physicians' group (the Harvey Society)—later published in *Medicine* in 1928—giving the medical community a clear epidemiologic and clinical picture of tularemia.[4] Other scientists often referred to his work on the disease as *Francis' baby* and tularemia was sometimes called *Francis' disease.* The pathogen responsible for the disease has also been called *Pasteurella tularensis,* a name Dr. Francis never accepted. The

Figure 2.2 Dr. Edward Francis worked closely with tularemia patients for 16 years, during which time he accidentally infected himself four times.

bacterium is now known as *Francisella tularensis* after a proposal by Russian scientists in 1959.

Dr. Francis **contracted** tularemia from the first deer-fly fever patient he visited in Utah. Sick for three months, he kept a careful record of his illness. He was continually exposed to *F. tularensis* for 16 years, accidentally re-infecting himself on four separate occasions. His writings stressed the high

EDWARD FRANCIS (1872–1952)

Dr. Edward Francis, who earned a B.S. from Ohio State University in 1894 and an M.D. from the University of Cincinnati in 1897, completed an internship at Cincinnati General Hospital and began his appointment as assistant surgeon with the United States Public Heath Service (USPHS) in 1900. He was appointed surgeon in 1912. In 1919, based out of the USPHS Hygienic Laboratory in Washington, D.C., he began his first field assignment studying deer-fly fever in Utah. He brought back infected animals to the Hygienic Laboratory, but was already sick with the disease from his trip to Utah.

In his laboratory, Dr. Francis isolated *Bacillus tularense* in animals, rabbit lice, bedbugs, and humans. Dr. Francis later described laboratory-acquired cases of a typhoidal type of tularemia (high fever, but no skin lesions) in laboratory scientists in 1922. He refined the anti-tularense agglutination test that allowed him to personally confirm 800 cases of human tularemia. It was in his summary published in *Medicine* in 1928 that clinical and epidemiologic features of a variety of forms of infection were identified as being, in fact, one infectious disease. By 1944, Dr. Francis confirmed 14,000 cases of tularemia in the United States.

He was nominated for a Nobel Prize in Physiology or Medicine in 1928, the same year he received a gold medal by the American Medical Association for a scientific exhibit of his research. Dr. Francis received two honorary doctoral degrees, one from Miami University in 1929 and one from his alma mater, Ohio State University, in 1933. He served with the USPHS from 1900 to 1938. Since 1959, the tularemia organism has been known as *Francisella* in honor of his tireless passion to unravel the story of tularemia as it unfolded in America.

Source: Jellison, W. L. "Tularemia" *Bulletins on the History of Medicine* 96(1972): 477–485.

occupational safety risk for scientific researchers working with *F. tularensis* in laboratory settings. His extensive research with the Hygienic Laboratory also contributed to his being infected with brucellosis, psittacosis, and relapsing fever over the course of his lengthy career.

Anti-tularense agglutination tests were developed by McCoy and Chapin and refined by Francis to improve the laboratory confirmation of *F. tularensis* infection in blood samples. What was thought to be several disparate infections was actually different clinical manifestations of infection with the same agent. Various occupational groups prone to acquiring the infection have been identified, and laboratory-acquired cases are still being reported. Various modes of transmission, such as contact with infected animals and arthropods, are associated with tularemia. These American experiences, recorded since the early 1900s, have made a significant contribution to the history of tularemia (Table 2.1).

3
Epidemiologic Trends

SOUTH DAKOTA OUTBREAK

In the summer of 1984, 28 Native Americans on the Lower Brule and Crow Creek Indian Reservations in central South Dakota experienced symptoms of tularemia after receiving tick bites.[1] The patients had mild symptoms that included fever, headache, and swelling at the site of the tick bites. An investigation identified ticks on vegetation in nearby streams. Many families had pet dogs and over 70% of the animals had tick infestations. These dog ticks, *Dermacentor variabilis*, tested positive for *F. tularensis*. Cases of tularemia were disproportionately high in the children on the reservation. In playing with the dogs, the children increased their exposure to the infected dog ticks. In addition, the children played in and around the streams and the vegetation where the infected ticks were abundant.

COMMON TYPES OF TULAREMIA

There are two main subtypes of *F. tularensis* associated with human tularemia. These are summarized in Table 3.1.

F. tularensis type A is found in North America, where it chiefly resides in rabbits and rodents. The bacterium moves from these sources of infection (reservoirs) with the help of ticks or deerflies, which act as vectors. The vectors carry the disease-causing bacterium to humans. Humans also come into contact with the pathogenic bacteria directly when handling infectious animals.

F. tularensis type B is seen in the United States but is also found in several other countries in the northern hemisphere. It is less virulent, takes considerably more bacteria to cause infection, and the resultant

Table 3.1 *Francisella tularensis* type A and B Causing Human Tularemia

Organism	Virulence	Occurrence	Source	Number of bacteria required to cause infection in humans	Severity
Francisella tularensis subspecies *tularensis* (refered to as sub-species *nearctica* in former Soviet Union) **Type A**	More virulent	Mainly North America	Reservoir in rabbits. Transmitted by ticks and deerflies.	10–50	Moderate to severe
Francisella tularensis subspecies *holarctica* (formerly subspecies *palaearctica*) **Type B**	Less virulent	Northern Hemisphere	Water and animals living near water.	12,000	Mild

Sources:
Saslaw, S., H. T. Eigelsbach, J. A. Prior, H. E. Wilson, and S. Carhart. "Tularemia Vaccine Study. II. Respiratory challenge." *Archives of Internal Medicine* 107(1961): 702–714.

Hornick, Richard. "Tularemia Revisited." *New England Journal of Medicine* 345(2001): 1637–1639.

Tärnvik, A., and L. Berglund. "Tularaemia." *European Respiratory Journal* 21(2003): 361–373.

disease is non-lethal. The bacterium can survive in water, swamps, and mud. *F. tularensis holarctica* is found in muskrats, voles, and rabbits that are infested with ticks and deerflies (and especially mosquitoes in Sweden). These animals can transmit the disease to humans through bites.

INCIDENCE OF TULAREMIA IN THE UNITED STATES
People of any age, sex, or race are susceptible to infection with *F. tularensis*. Since the early 1950s, there has been a steep

decrease in the number of human tularemia cases each year in the United States.

From a high of 2,291 cases in 1939, there are now only 100 to 200 cases on average in a given year. This is attributable to a decline in reliance on hunting and trapping and, thus, exposure to natural reservoirs like the cottontail, marsh, and swamp rabbits.

Ticks and deerflies are common sources of human infection in the United States, transmitting *F. tularensis* through their bites. Trend data indicate that these exposures continue to be significant forms of transmission in the United States.

UNITED STATES GEOGRAPHIC DISTRIBUTION OF TULAREMIA

Annual cases of tularemia are scattered across the United States but occur most prominently in the central region (Figure 3.1).

On this map, we can also see the year 2000 outbreak on Martha's Vineyard in Massachusetts (see Chapter 7). The U.S. geographic distribution reveals that four states accounted for over 50% of all tularemia cases between 1990 and 2000: Arkansas, Missouri, South Dakota, and Oklahoma (Table 3.2).

In Arkansas and Missouri, where over 40% of U.S. cases of tularemia occur, the source of infection was tick bites (e.g., in 76% of Arkansas cases). Tularemia cases increase in summer months (e.g., 56% of all cases in Arkansas are between May and July). Data on six Southwestern-Central states (Arkansas, Kansas, Louisiana, Missouri, Oklahoma, and Texas) from 1981 to 1987 showed that the main clinical presentations were fever (96%), **lymphadenitis** (77%), and skin **ulcers** (65%).[2] Most tularemia cases were white (88%) males (75%) with a median age of 40 years. The case-fatality rate was 2%, but higher when adjusted for age over 50 years (4.8% versus 0.4% for under 50 years).

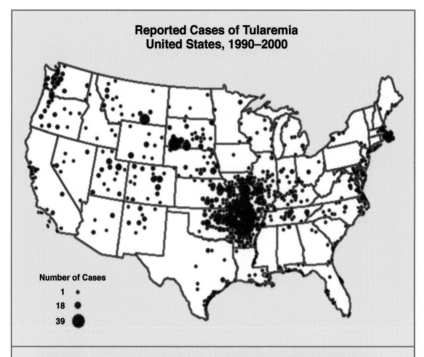

**Reported Cases of Tularemia
United States, 1990–2000**

Number of Cases

1

18

39

Figure 3.1 This map shows the distribution of reported cases of tularemia in the United States from 1990 to 2000. A strong concentration of cases appears in the central region of the country, with over 40% of U.S. cases occurring in Missouri and Arkansas.

SEASONAL DISTRIBUTION AND SOURCE OF EXPOSURE

More cases of tularemia occur in the summer months than the winter months. In fact, the seasonal distribution of cases corresponds with the summer peak of the tick population. We know that tick bites and deerfly bites are a significant source of infection in the United States. Thirty-eight percent of cases in Oklahoma, and only 10% in Arkansas, attribute their source of exposure as contact with rabbits, whereas 68% of cases in the Southwest-Central region report a tick bite prior to the onset of their symptoms. Ticks have replaced rabbits as the most frequently reported source of exposure by tularemia patients.

Table 3.2 Four States with the Highest Tularemia Incidence, United States 1990–2000.

High Tularemia Incidence by State	Number of Cases	Percent of U.S. Cases
Arkansas	315	23%
Missouri	265	19%
South Dakota	96	7%
Oklahoma	90	7%

Source: *MMWR* "Tularemia–United States, 1990–2000." March 8, 2002.51(9); 182–184.

Oklahoma cases between 1979 and 1985, plotted by month, show a peak (55% of cases) from tick exposure in the months May through July. A second peak in cases occurred from October to December, which coincides with the Oklahoma rabbit-hunting season (October 1 through March 15) and accounted for 38% of all cases.

From year to year, the number of cases associated with tick exposure is fairly constant. The cases per year resulting from exposure to infected rabbits changes with the total number of rabbits harvested in Oklahoma.

A disproportionate number of cases occur in the Native American population of the United States. Between 1992 and 1999, the Notifiable Diseases Surveillance System attributed

10% of tularemia cases to persons who identified themselves as Native Americans. Data from this set may underreport tularemia, since the disease was not a nationally **notifiable disease** between 1995 and 1998. Additionally, there is under-reporting for less severe cases who do not seek medical treatment, are not hospitalized, or do not have laboratory confirmation of their condition.

TULAREMIA IN CHILDREN

Most reported cases of tularemia occur in adults, but recent data examined from the Notifiable Diseases Surveillance System between 1992 and 1999 showed the highest rates of tularemia occurred in children one to 14 years of age. The 1984 outbreak of 28 cases involving children on the Lower Brule and Crow Creek Indian Reservations followed similar outbreaks of 12 cases in 1979 on the Crow Indian Reservation in Montana and 12 cases in 1966 on the Pine Ridge and Rosebud Indian Reservations in South Dakota. These childhood tularemia infections caused mild symptoms of fever, headache, and swollen glands.

Investigators found that children's exposure to tularemia occurred from contact with pet dogs infested with tularemia-infected ticks and from playing in muddy, wet areas that were confirmed in laboratory tests to be reservoirs for tularemia. The children had a different pattern of risk than the adults, stemming from their exposure patterns from playing.

WORLDWIDE DISTRIBUTION

Worldwide, the distribution of tularemia is primarily concentrated in the northern hemisphere. Tularemia is **endemic** in regions between the latitudes of 30° and 71° north: North America, Scandinavian countries, Russia, Europe, Japan, and China.

Tularemia bacteria can survive for long periods in mud and cold water. Contaminated water continues to be an important environmental source of tularemia. In the summer of 1998, an explosion in the crayfish population at the neck of the Buendia Dam (14 km from the town of Huete, Spain) allowed men and women who were crayfishing that July to just reach in and grab crayfish in the muddy sediment. Normally, these fishing enthusiasts would use nets, but in 1998 they just used

EPIDEMIOLOGY, BIOGEOGRAPHY, GEOGRAPHIC INFORMATION SYSTEMS (GIS), AND WILLIAM L. JELLISON

Spot mapping has a long and distinguished history from the earliest days of epidemiologic investigation. In London in 1854, John Snow placed a black dot on a map for each residence in which a fatality from cholera occurred in certain sub-districts of the city. From this spot map of the geographic distribution of cholera deaths, Snow was convinced of a connection between the cholera cases and sources of drinking water.

With tularemia, there was William Jellison, a parasitologist who in 1950 correlated the geographical distribution of the deerfly species *Chrysops discalis* with the incidence of tularemia in humans. He acknowledged Edward Francis and B. Mayne for identifying *Chrysops discalis* as an efficient experimental vector in their laboratory. Jellison sought to show an association in nature between one species of *Chrysops discalis* and tularemia incidence in humans.

Jellison's use of **biogeography** provided circumstantial evidence that *Chrysops discalis* was the deerfly of "deer-fly fever." Human tularemia occurred in the geographic zone common to *C. discalis*, despite the predominance of 68 species and 12 subspecies of the genus *Chrysops* in North America; Jellison postulated that *C. discalis'* predilection for feeding primarily on rabbits and rodents their hands even though the skin on their hands was cut in the process.

It had been less than a year since the 1997 outbreak of 585 cases of hare-associated ulceroglandular tularemia in Spain, so awareness of the disease was still high. When persons with ulcerated sores on their hands, swollen glands, and fever

defined its role as a natural vector of *F. tularensis* in human tularemia.

The first isolation of *F. tularensis* from deerflies (in the absence of human cases of tularemia) was in 1964. In 1973, Lawrence Klock published the close temporal association of *F. tularensis* infected *Chrysops discalis* with a large human tularemia outbreak from deerfly bites.

Currently, geographic information systems (GIS) are an integral tool in observational epidemiology. Geographical mapping helps ongoing surveillance, investigations of outbreaks, and establishing predictive patterns that assist in the development of preventive measures of public health and medical treatment. The CDC National Center for Health Statistics promotes GIS in public health, making available information, maps, and links to related sites.

Sources:

Klock, L. E., P. F. Olsen, T. Fukushima. "Tularemia Epidemic Associated with the Deerfly." *JAMA* 226(2)(1973): 149–152.

Jellison, William L. "Tularemia. Geographic Distribution of 'Deerfly Fever' and the Biting Fly, *Chrysops discalis*." *Public Health Reports* 65 (October 13, 1950): 1321–1329.

Thorpe, B. B., et al. "Tularemia in Wildlife and Livestock of the Great Salt Lake Desert Region, 1951–1964." *American Journal of Tropical Medicine and Hygiene* 14(1965): 622–637.

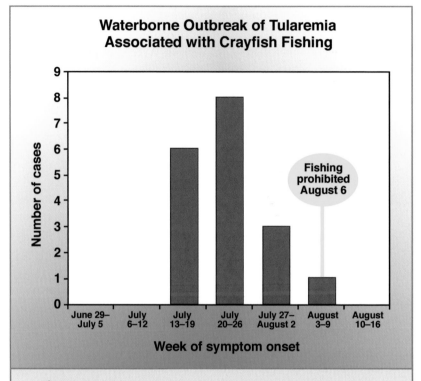

Figure 3.2 This graph shows the distribution of tularemia cases by onset date of symptoms during an outbreak in Spain in the summer of 1998. Nineteen cases were laboratory confirmed (one case had an unknown onset date of symptoms). The graph highlights that prohibition of crayfish fishing on August 6, 1998 halted further exposure.

showed up at medical offices, the 1998 outbreak was quickly identified as tularemia.[3] Nineteen cases were laboratory confirmed between July 13 and July 31, 1998. Six of these cases had ulcers on their fingers and the remaining persons had **inflammation** from crayfishing injuries. One case arose from an **abrasion** from a riverbank reed, which caused a **lesion** at the site of the scratch and, as with the others, ultimately led to infection with *F. tularensis* type B. No insect bites were reported in these crayfisher cases (Figure 3.2).

Since crayfish accumulate toxins from their water habitats, dissected tissue from the crayfish livers was examined. The results were positive for *F. tularensis*. Water samples taken upstream near a sewage plant discharge pipe one month after the outbreak also tested positive for *F. tularensis*. Finding *F. tularensis* in the crayfish and in the water established the **ecological** source of this outbreak as waterborne.

4

Tularemia Diseases

The history of tick-bite, fly-bite, or wild rabbit contact especially, or contact with other animals, when coupled with fever, an ulcer on the skin, and regional lymph-node enlargement, should call attention to tularemia. Diagnosis is made conclusive by obtaining agglutination of *Bacterium tularense* by the patient's serum or by obtaining a culture of the organism from the patient's ulcer or lymph nodes following guinea pig inoculation. . . . [1]

PATHOPHYSIOLOGY OF TULAREMIA

Tularemia is always characterized by fever. Two main factors that determine the particular clinical form of tularemia in a person exposed to *F. tularensis* are the infecting strain and the portal of entry.

The most common portals of entry are insect bites in the lower extremities or contact with an infected animal on the hands or upper body. Less than 10 virulent bacteria (when injected) or 10 to 50 bacteria (when inhaled) have been shown in experiments with volunteers to produce clinical tularemia in humans.

F. tularensis reproduces locally at the site of infection in the body for two to five days. A visible sore or lesion often arises at the site of entry of the bacteria, usually a red sore with a ribbed rim. The red sore may have a punched-out center. In ulceroglandular forms of tularemia, *F. tularensis* spreads into the **lymph nodes** in the immediate vicinity of the entry point, producing a bulbous swelling of the lymph nodes (lymphadenitis) that can range from 1 to 10 cm in diameter. If the bacteria enter the bloodstream (causing **bacteremia**), the infection can proceed into the lungs, spleen, liver, and kidneys.[2] In some instances, tularemia causes **meningitis**, a swelling of the membranes surrounding the brain and spinal cord.

People can also be exposed to aerosolized *F. tularensis*, usually from an occupational exposure. When the bacteria are inhaled, the person develops hemorrhagic **inflammation** of the airways that can progress to **bronchopneumonia,** in which the air sacs in the lungs fill with cells and fluid from the immune system. Untreated tularemia **pneumonia** has a 60% fatality rate; therefore, early diagnosis and treatment with **antibiotics** is vitally important.

Typhoidal tularemia occurs without any skin ulcer or lesions, and the lymph nodes swell very little (less than 1 cm in diameter), but the patient appears septic with a high fever. These patients often have pneumonia. This is the hardest form of the disease to diagnose without a specific link to a source of tularemia infection or a positive laboratory test. With typhoidal tularemia, it is likely that the patient's infection will become fatal.

DESCRIPTION OF *F. TULARENSIS*: THE BACTERIUM

A staining procedure known as Gram staining is often used to help identify types of bacteria. A purple dye (crystal violet) is used on a blood sample. If the bacteria within the blood sample retain the crystal violet color in their cell walls they are labeled **gram-positive**. If, after staining, the bacterial cell wall loses the violet color and ends up looking light red, the bacteria are considered **gram-negative**. *F. tularensis* is a gram-negative bacterium (Figure 4.1).

F. tularensis is small (measuring only 0.2 to 0.5 micrometers by 0.7 to 1.0 micrometers) and rod-shaped (coccobacillus). These bacteria are difficult to see by a light microscope in blood or tissue samples (Figure 4.2).

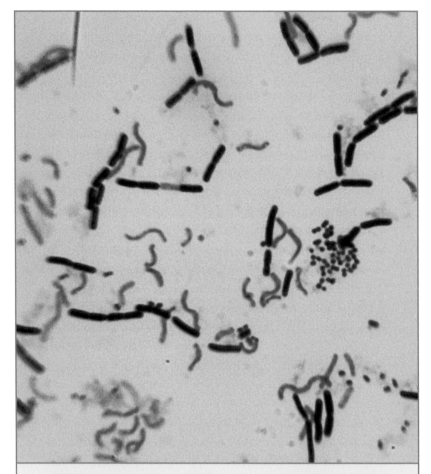

Figure 4.1 A Gram stain is often used to identify bacteria. If the bacterium retains a crystal violet color, it is labeled gram-positive. If the bacterium appears light red after staining, as *F. tularensis* does, it is gram-negative. This bacteria is considered gram-negative.

REPLICATION AND CONTROL

F. tularensis reproduces **aerobically** (needing oxygen). It is an intracellular pathogen, which means that it directly enters host cells to replicate. *F. tularensis* lives as a **parasite** within **macrophages**, a particular type of cell that makes up the body's immune response to bacterial infection. Macrophages engulf

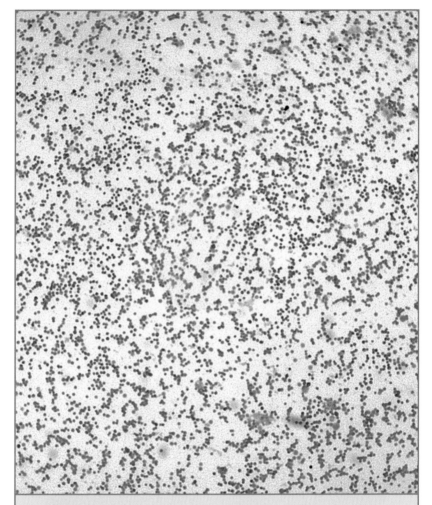

Figure 4.2 This is an image of *F. tularensis*, a very small and rod-shaped bacteria. It is difficult to detect in blood or tissue samples.

and destroy bacteria in a process called **phagocytosis**. However, *F. tularensis* can survive phagocytosis and replicate for long periods of time in the body, leading to a long, drawn-out illness in the infected person.

In the laboratory, *F. tularensis* is difficult to culture. It grows poorly on standard growth media but will grow on media enriched with the amino acid cysteine. Tularemia is susceptible to a group of antibiotics: aminoglycosides (*i.e.,* streptomycin, gentamicin), tetracycline, fluoroquinolones, and chloramphenicol. Physicians usually prescribe streptomycin and gentamicin to treat patients with tularemia.

CLINICAL FORMS OF TULAREMIA

Tularemia was originally classified into two major clinical forms: ulceroglandular and typhoidal. Now several distinguishable forms are known.

Ulceroglandular tularemia accounts for 75% to 85% of tularemia cases. It is characterized by a break in the skin that becomes inflamed (ulcerative) within a few days after infection occurs. Sixty percent of sores develop ulcers that are 0.4 to 3 cm in diameter and have heaped up edges. The ulcer on the skin of a patient may only be noticed by the examining physician (Figure 4.3).

Handling infected animals can cause infections in the skin of the hands or produce lesions on the upper extremities. Tick bites are seen primarily on the lower extremities in adults. In adults, the lymph nodes in the groin are most commonly affected. In children, ticks bites to the head and neck area are common, accompanied by swollen lymph nodes in the neck.

Swollen lymph nodes greater than 1 cm in diameter are very prominent in 85% of patients. It is often from the tender and obviously swollen lymph nodes that infected persons seek medical treatment. Lymph glands may need to be drained by **needle aspiration** following treatment with antibiotics. The swollen lymph gland is at risk of rupture (**abscess**) or can become ulcerative (Figure 4.4).

Glandular tularemia is the second most common form of the disease and also includes swollen lymph nodes (lymphadenitis). A local site of infection is not apparent.

Oculoglandular tularemia cases occur in patients who have spread the infection to their eyes by rubbing them with

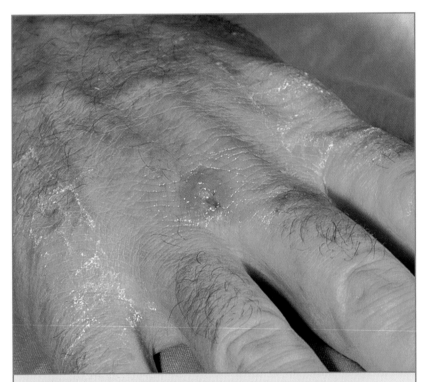

Figure 4.3 Symptoms of tularemia vary depending on how the person was initially exposed. Insect bites or abrasions can be points of entry for the *F. tularensis* bacteria into the body. Ulcerated lesions, such as this case on the dorsal skin of the right hand of a patient, are caused by infection with *F. tularensis*.

fingers contaminated with *F. tularensis*. Contamination by a tick or a particle in the air can also lead to oculoglandular tularemia. Oculoglandular tularemia is characterized by painful ulceration in the white part (conjunctiva) of the eye and swelling of regional lymph nodes.

Oropharyngeal tularemia occurs from consuming contaminated water or food, or from putting infected fingers into the mouth. This form of tularemia produces an infected pharynx, possible pharyngeal ulceration, swollen lymph glands in the neck, severe throat pain, nausea, and vomiting.

The diagnosis can be missed by physicians when there is no clear link to a source of tularemia. Lymph node abscesses occur in up to 40% of infected patients who are not given timely diagnosis and treatment.

Typhoidal tularemia is a systemic illness that is present without a localized site of infection. Lymph node swelling is less than 1 cm. This is the hardest clinical form of tularemia to diagnose. The patient has fever, severe headache, and sometimes low blood pressure. Eighty percent of typhoidal

THE LYMPH SYSTEM

The lymph system is part of the immune system and is intimately connected to the circulatory system (See figure). Lymph vessels extend into tissues throughout the body. The main function of the lymphatic system is collecting and transporting fluid from spaces between tissues of the body to the veins of the circulatory system. Bean-shaped lymph nodes located throughout the system store **lymphocytes** that help filter out and destroy foreign organisms.

When people who are sick say that they have swollen glands, they usually mean swollen lymph nodes. The lymph nodes act as local storage areas for **antibodies** and **leukocytes**. They are situated in both armpits, above the shoulder bone, in the neck, in the groin area, and in back of the head just above hairline. They become very swollen when leukocytes fight infection. When they fight bacterial infections, the person is said to have lymphadenitis.

This illustration (right) shows the major components of the lymphatic system: lymphatic vessels, lymph nodes, and other lymphatic organs. Bean-shaped lymph nodes, which store antibodies and leukocytes, become swollen when leukocytes fight infection.

tularemia patients get pneumonia (versus 30% with ulcer-oglandular tularemia).

Pulmonary, **pneumonic**, or **inhalation tularemia** occurs when *F. tularensis* is inhaled and directly enters the patient's lungs. The bacterium can be aerosolized unintentionally by disturbing dirt mounds made by infected voles in farm fields, by cutting fields in which infected animal droppings are located, or by moving bales of hay containing tularemia bacteria. From 25% to 30% of patients with

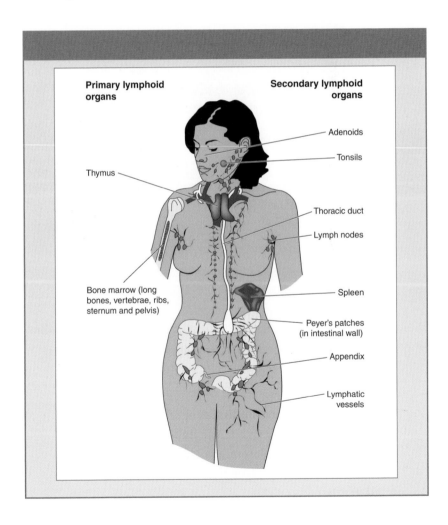

Primary lymphoid organs

Secondary lymphoid organs

Adenoids

Tonsils

Thymus

Thoracic duct

Lymph nodes

Bone marrow (long bones, vertebrae, ribs, sternum and pelvis)

Spleen

Peyer's patches (in intestinal wall)

Appendix

Lymphatic vessels

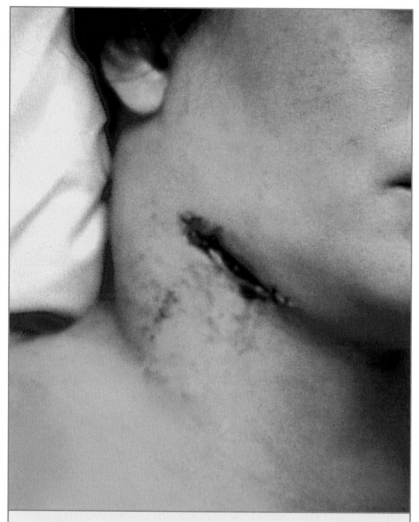

Figure 4.4 This photo shows a patient with ulcerating lymphadenitis caused by tularemia.

this form of disease have **infiltrates** of cells and fluid seen on lung X-rays without any clinical findings of pneumonia. An inhaled form of tularemia is also the likeliest disease to arise from any intentional bioterrorism attack using *F. tularensis.*

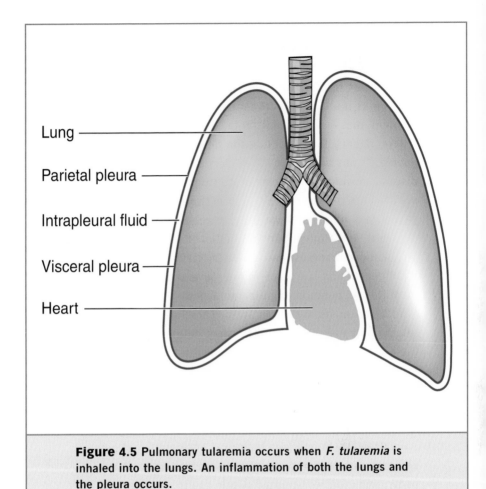

Lung

Parietal pleura

Intrapleural fluid

Visceral pleura

Heart

Figure 4.5 Pulmonary tularemia occurs when *F. tularemia* is inhaled into the lungs. An inflammation of both the lungs and the pleura occurs.

An inflammation of both the lungs and covering of the lungs (pleura) occurs. The pneumonia arising from the inhalation of bacteria is serious enough that the patient requires assistance by mechanical ventilation to breathe. Pulmonary fluid that accumulates in the pleural space causes **pleural effusion** that is seen on patient X-rays (Figure 4.5). Before antibiotics were available, *F. tularensis* type A inhalation tularemia that caused pneumonia resulted in death in 30% to 60% of infected persons.

CATEGORIES OF BIOLOGICAL TERRORISM AGENTS

The Centers for Disease Control and Prevention (CDC, a division of the U.S. Department of Health and Human Services that is based in Atlanta, Georgia) is the lead federal agency for protecting the health and safety of people. It has a strong national focus on developing disease prevention and control strategies, as well as maintaining disease surveillance networks.

From a June 1999 meeting between the Department of Health and Human Services staff and national experts in infectious diseases, public health, civilian and military intelligence, and law enforcement, several organisms were identified as potential high-impact agents that could be used by terrorists in civilian areas. Three classification levels—Categories A, B, and C—were defined, with A being the highest level of adverse public health impact with mass casualties, high potential for mass dissemination, and a level of heightened awareness that would lead to mass panic. The table on page 47 summarizes the three categories of biological terrorism agents.

Category A contains biological organisms that can be easily disseminated, cause mass casualties and/or panic, and require increased public health preparedness (such as improved surveillance, laboratory diagnosis, and stockpiling of specific medications).

Category B includes agents that can be easily spread, have an impact on community health (morbidity), have a low risk of death (mortality), and require enhanced disease surveillance.

Category C are agents that can be engineered by terrorists intent on spreading disease, due to their availability, ease of production, and potential for morbidity and mortality.

CATEGORIES OF BIOLOGICAL TERRORISM AGENTS

Category	Disease	Biological Terrorism Agent
A	Smallpox	Variola major virus
A	Anthrax	*Bacillus anthracis*
A	Plague	*Yersinia pestis*
A	Botulism	*Clostridium botulinum*
A	Tularemia	*Francisella tularensis*
A	Viral hemorrhagic fevers	Filoviruses Arenaviruses (e.g., Ebola and Lassa viruses)
B	Q Fever	*Coxiella burnetii*
B	Brucellosis	*Brucella spp.*
B	Glanders	*Burkholderia mallei*
B	Melioidosis	*Burkholderia pseudomallei*
B	Encephalitis	Eastern equine encephalitis virus Western equine encephalitis virus Venezuelen equine encephalitis virus
B	Toxic syndromes	Toxins (e.g., *Clostridium perfringens*, Staphylococcal enterotoxin B, Ricin)
B	Typhus fever	*Rickettsia prowazekii*
B	Cholera	*Vibrio cholerae*
B	Psittacosis	*Chlamydia psittaci*
B	Shigellosis	*Shigella dysenteriae*
B	*E. coli*	*Escherichia coli* O157:H7
B	*Salmonella*	*Salmonella spp.*
B	*Cryptosporidium*	*Cryptosporidium parvum*
C	Emerging threats	Nipah virus, hantavirus, Tickborne hemorrhagic fever viruses, Tickborne encephalitis viruses, Yellow fever virus, multidrug-resistant *Mycobacterium tuberculosis*

Sources:

Nolte, K, B. Randy L. Hanzlick, et al. "Medical Examiners, Coroners, and Bioterrorism: A Guidebook for Surveillance and Case Management." *MMWR* 53(RR-8)(2004): 1–27.

Rotz, L., A. S. Khan, S. R. Lillibridge, S. M. Ostroff, J. M. Hughes. "Public Health Assessment of Potential Biological Terrorism Agents." *Emerging Infectious Diseases* 8(2)(February 2002): 225–230.

5

Diagnosis and Medical Treatment

The diagnosis of tularemia is complicated by the fact that tularemia is very rare, with fewer than 200 cases per year in the United States. Patients can present to their physician with symptoms that resemble other diseases; these other diseases would first have to be ruled out. If the person is not in or has not recently visited an area where tularemia is endemic, the doctor will likely have trouble identifying his or her symptoms as a case of tularemia.

Central to reaching an accurate diagnosis is obtaining a clear medical history from the patient, particularly regarding any association he or she may recall to possible sources of tularemia infection. Such events could be contact with rabbits (eating, handling, skinning, tanning, or hunting), exposure to ticks, or recent travel to areas where tularemia is endemic.

Although the index of suspicion for a diagnosis of tularemia in affected hunters, trappers, veterinarians, and laboratory workers should be high, 40% of tularemia cases have no known link to contact with a source of tularemia infection. An ulcerative skin lesion and dramatic lymph node swelling provide excellent clues to the diagnosis of ulceroglandular tularemia (over 75% of naturally occurring tularemia cases). Typhoidal tularemia and pneumonic tularemia are much more difficult to diagnose. Delays to the diagnosis prevent prompt treatment of the disease and may mean extra weeks of failing health for the patient.

DIFFERENTIAL DIAGNOSIS
There are many diseases that resemble the conditions presented by

tularemia patients that the physician needs to rule out for a presumptive diagnosis. The process of ruling out other similar diseases is called the **differential diagnosis**. Table 5.1 illustrates the similarities that the different forms of tularemia have with many other serious diseases.

EVIDENCE OF *F. TULARENSIS* INFECTION

Direct microscopic examination to identify *F. tularensis* in patient samples is extremely difficult, since the bacterium is very small. Gram stain tests, which are automatically performed on patient fluids (like sputum), are often obscured by background material that make the weakly staining tularemia bacterium not readily distinguishable. Another rapid diagnostic procedure is the microscopic observation of *F. tularensis* in patient blood, secretions, or biopsy material using fluorescent-labeled antibodies (Figure 5.1). This test is available in designated reference laboratories (usually state public health laboratories). Fluorescent antibody tests can be useful, but false-positive results due to similarities between *F. tularensis* and *Legionella spp.* have been reported.

Confirmation of a case of tularemia (by the Centers for Disease Control and Prevention, or CDC) relies on the direct isolation of *F. tularensis*.[1] Tularemia bacteria can be cultured from a sample taken from a skin ulcer, a lymph node aspirate, gastric wash, or sputum. *F. tularensis* differs from most bacteria in that it requires cysteine-glucose-blood agar to grow in culture. With a heavy inoculum load, the bacterium can grow in an 18-hour period. Bacterial culture, for safety reasons, requires biohazard level 3 facilities for isolation. It is one of the most common laboratory-acquired infections in unvaccinated laboratory workers in the United States. Due to the constraints with culturing, few clinical laboratories have experience isolating *F. tularensis*. Laboratories with little experience of cultivating *F. tularensis* may not succeed in correctly identifying it,

Table 5.1 Differential Diagnosis of Tularemia Infection

Tularemia Presentation (accompanied by fever)	Differential Diagnosis
Ulceroglandular-Skin ulcer with lymphadenitis	Skin infection with *Streptococcus pyogenes* or *Staphylococcus aureus*, spider bite, rickettsialpox, syphilis, *Pasteurella* infections, or cutaneous anthrax
Glandular-Lymphadenitis without skin ulcer	Pyogenic bacterial infection, cat scratch disease, syphilis, tuberculosis, or plague
Oculoglandular-Acute conjunctivitis with swelling	Pyogenic bacterial infection, adenoviral infection, syphilis, cat scratch disease, mycobacterium tuberculosis, coccidiomycosis, or herpes infection
Pharyngeal-Tonsillitis with ulcer	Infectious mononucleosis, pharyngitis, diphtheria, or adenovirus
Typhoidal-Systemic involvement	Typhoid fever, Q fever, leptospirosis, malaria, brucellosis, rickettsiosis, or fungal infection
Pneumonic-Acute inflammation	Community-acquired pneumonia, *Coxiella burnetii*, *Legionella pneumophila*, *Chlamydia psittaci*, anthrax, *Mycobacterium tuberculosis*, pneumonic plague, or viral pneumonias such as hantavirus pulmonary syndrome, respiratory syncytial virus, influenza, or cytomegalovirus

Source: Nolte, K. B., *et al*. "Medical Examiners, Coroners, and Bioterrorism: A Guidebook for Surveillance and Case Management." MMWR. June 11, 2004. vol.53. No. RR-8. pp.1–27.

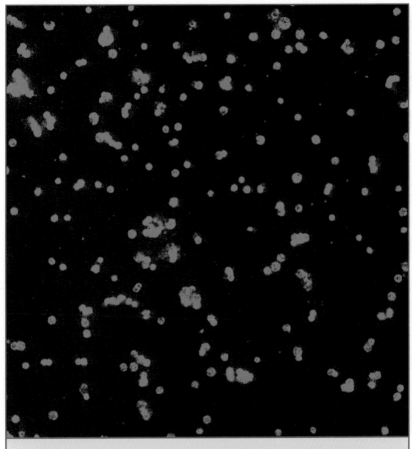

Figure 5.1 This is an image of *Francisella tularensis* shown under a microscope at 1000x magnification, with direct fluorescent antibody stain (DFA). DFA is a rapid diagnostic test that uses fluorescent-labeled antibodies to observe bacteria in patient samples.

since traditional biochemical testing is of little value in identification.

Antibody detection is the key laboratory evaluation tool for identifying *F. tularensis* infection after it is clinically suspected. Testing patients' blood for antibodies against *F. tularensis*, for example by using an agglutination test (Chapter 2), can also be used to confirm tularemia.

Confirmation comes from detecting a fourfold or higher increase of agglutinating antibodies between an initial blood sample and one taken 10 to 14 days later, reflecting the body's continued development of an antibody response to *F. tularensis* infection.

In 1967, over one thousand people became infected with airborne tularemia in Northern Sweden. Fifty-four infected patients from this outbreak were tracked in a

ELISA

An enzyme-linked immunosorbant assay (ELISA) is used to test for infection with *F. tularensis* (See figure). Cultures of the bacteria are mixed with detergents to extract outer membrane proteins. These proteins are used to coat plastic 96-well ELISA plates. Blood serum from patients suspected of having tularemia is diluted and placed into specific wells on the plate. If the patient has antibodies that bind to *F. tularensis* proteins, these antibodies will stick to the wells and not be washed away. These antibodies will be bound by an enzyme-linked second antibody that binds specifically to human antibodies. Adding the enzyme's substrate to each well of the plate will generate a colored reaction only if antibodies to *F. tularensis* proteins are present in the blood sample. The same color intensity seen in a fourfold more dilute sample taken two to three weeks later from the same patient, representing a rise in antibody concentration in the blood, helps to confirm a case of active infection with *F. tularensis*.

The ELISA test detects a person's antibodies to *F. tularensis*. The diagram (right) shows that positive results are indicated by a colored reaction.

research study to evaluate the persistence of tularemia antibodies in their bloodstream over time. Twenty-five years after the outbreak, all of the original 54 patients were retested for tularemia antibodies and still had positive agglutination tests (a titer of ≥1:80 by the tube agglutination test, meaning that blood diluted 80-fold or greater was still able to clump *F. tularensis* bacteria together).[2] The Swedish study confirmed the long persistence of anti-tularense

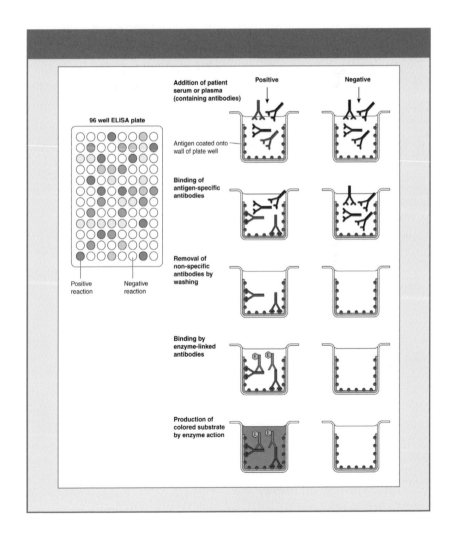

antibodies and highlights the fact that a **false-positive** result can occur without recent exposure. It emphasizes the need to demonstrate a fourfold rise in antibody titer to confirm an acute infection.

During the past decade, agglutination testing has been less favored compared to the enzyme-linked immunosorbent assay (**ELISA**) test. ELISA is 10 times more sensitive than agglutination tests.[3] Agglutination relies on clumping of the whole bacterium with antibodies in the patient's blood sample. ELISA instead relies on purified protein components of the bacterium's outer membrane to attract and bind the patient's antibodies. The trapped antibodies are then detected with a secondary antibody linked to an enzyme that develops a colored reaction.

DNA-based polymerase chain reaction (PCR) tests are effective in detecting *F. tularensis* even after initiation of antibiotic treatment in the patient. Recent evaluation of samples once collected during epidemics in Sweden in 1995 and 1998 have shown that PCR is more sensitive than culturing *F. tularensis*. PCR detected *F. tularensis* DNA in 75% of patients having culture- and/or serology-verified ulceroglandular tularemia. All kinds of tissues, including ulcerated skin tissue, can be used in PCR detection. New research has shown that PCR is valuable for earlier diagnosis of tularemia and even in the typing of specific *F. tularensis* strains. However, it is not yet available in most public health laboratories.

TREATMENT

Virtually all strains of *F. tularensis* can be treated by the antibiotic streptomycin. It is considered the first-line therapy for tularemia. Since it was first developed in 1947, streptomycin has proven 97% effective in treating tularemia infections. Streptomycin injections are given intramuscularly (7.5 mg/kg of patient body weight) every 12 hours for a

(continued on page 58)

INVENTION OF PCR

The amplification of deoxyribonucleic acid (DNA) molecules requires a few ingredients: two short DNA primers, which flank the beginning and end of the DNA sequence of interest; DNA building blocks; and a heat-stable enzyme DNA polymerase, which reads and assembles the blocks. In the presence of heat, the sequence is transcribed faithfully, generating successive copies of the original strand. Dr. Kary Mullis made the polymerase chain reaction (PCR) technique a commercialized scientific tool. Dr. Mullis conceived of PCR in 1983 and received the Nobel Prize in Physiology or Medicine for his invention in 1993. Today, PCR has many commercial and medical applications, some of which are listed in the Table on page 56.

PCR is useful for *F. tularensis* identification because this bacterium is known to be difficult and hazardous to culture and its small size makes it hard to see under a microscope. PCR can generate 100 billion copies of the original DNA molecule in a matter of hours.

The PCR technique begins with collection of the patient sample. Due to the extreme sensitivity of PCR in amplification, contamination is a common problem and is best solved by having samples collected using sterile (aseptic) techniques with disposable plastic tools into sterile sealed bags.

The complementary strands of double-stranded DNA within *F. tularensis* are separated by heating. Two small pieces of synthetic DNA, each complementary to a specific sequence in the *F. tularensis* target sequence, serve as **primers**. Each primer binds to its complementary sequence. The heat stable DNA polymerase starts at each primer and copies the sequence of that strand. Within a short time, exact replicas of the target sequence have been produced.

INVENTION OF PCR *(continued)*

Current Uses of PCR

Used by the food industry to check the origin species of meat in order to validate its purity.

Food industry checks for traces of peanuts in food products to validate ingredient list.

Tissue and blood samples at the scene of a crime can be amplified and compared to potential suspects.

Genetic tests can identify inherited disorders, as well as people who carry a mutation that can be passed to their children, allowing for genetic counseling.

PCR can amplify organisms' genomic DNA in a patient sample to allow identification of the pathogen.

In subsequent heat cycles, double-stranded molecules of both the original DNA and the copies are separated; primers bind again to their complementary sequences and the polymerase replicates them. At the end of many cycles, the PCR reaction is greatly enriched in the small pieces of DNA that have the target sequences, and this amplified genetic information is then available for further analysis and detection (See figure).

Source: Sjostedt, A., U. Eriksson, L. Berglund, A. Tarnvik. "Detection of *Francisella tularensis* in Ulcers of Patients with Tularemia by PCR." *Journal of Clinical Microbiology* 35(1997): 1045–1048.

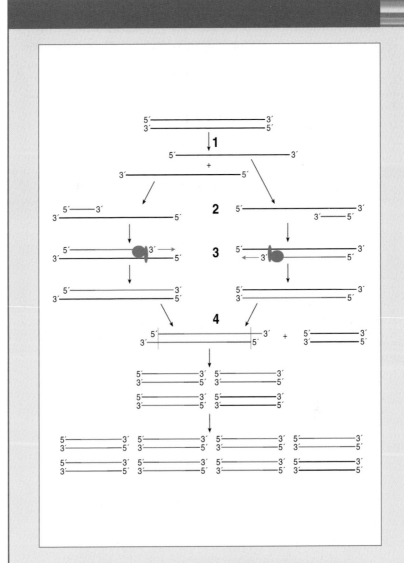

In the polymerase chain reaction, a DNA template is copied through repeated steps of (1) denaturing (separation) by heat, (2) annealing (binding) of short DNA primers, and (3) extending the primers using DNA polymerase, leading to (4) an extension of the original template.

(continued from page 54)

10- to 14-day course of treatment. It may take one or two weeks for skin lesions to heal and for lymph node swelling to subside.

Gentamicin is another effective therapy against tularemia. Pregnant women should use gentamicin instead of streptomycin, as streptomycin can cause deafness in the developing fetus. Other drugs of choice include doxycycline and ciprofloxacin.

HOW DOES STREPTOMYCIN ACTUALLY WORK?

Streptomycin is in the aminoglycoside family of antibiotics. It is not absorbed if ingested orally, so it must be given by **intramuscular injection** to the mid-thigh or gluteus maximus (the rear end).

All members of the aminoglycoside antibiotic family are well known for their potential to cause permanent ear poisoning (ototoxicity) if they enter the inner ear.

Since streptomycin can cause toxicity in the fetus, it is not recommended for pregnant women.

Absorption from intramuscular injection is rapid, with peak blood levels achieved within one hour. If the patient has kidney (renal) impairment, the streptomycin does not get excreted properly from the body and accumulates, causing renal toxicity. There is a fine line between streptomycin being therapeutic and being toxic, so careful attention must be paid to dosage calculations.

Streptomycin actually works by creating a barrier to the bacterium's new synthesis of proteins through the translation of messenger RNA (mRNA). Streptomycin binds to the ribosomal RNA component of the 30S ribosome subunit in *F. tularensis*. This binding prevents the proper translation of mRNA into protein, leading over time to the death of the bacterium (See figure).

Patients with pneumonic tularemia may also require supportive respiratory care. Patients with ulceroglandular tularemia need moist bandages for their skin sores that require frequent changing. Patients with lymphadenitis who require pus to be drained should receive several days of streptomycin therapy first to prevent the medical staff performing the draining procedure (aspiration) from becoming exposed to *F. tularensis* infection themselves.

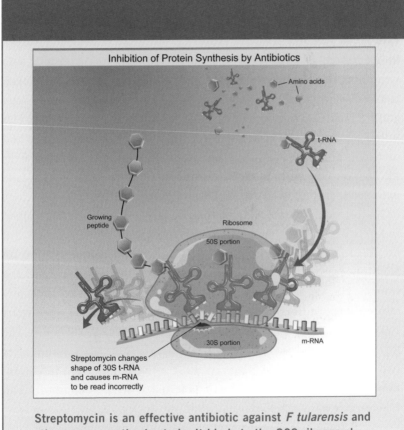

Inhibition of Protein Synthesis by Antibiotics

Amino acids

t-RNA

Growing peptide

Ribosome

50S portion

Streptomycin changes shape of 30S t-RNA and causes m-RNA to be read incorrectly

30S portion

m-RNA

Streptomycin is an effective antibiotic against *F tularensis* and other gram-negative bacteria. It binds to the 30S ribosomal RNA subunit and changes its shape causing protein synthesis to be altered.

6

Arthropod and Animal Transmission

THE NEW JERSEY RABBIT HUNTER

In late November 1985, a 67-year-old woman went to the hospital with symptoms of dehydration, **sepsis**, and a lingering sore on her finger. Her young neighbor had hunted rabbits in early November, and—after gutting them—gave two rabbits to her and her husband to skin. Her initial treatment on November 23, 1985 was with gentamicin and cefazolin. Three days later, she was given streptomycin. Unfortunately, she died on December 3, 1985.[1] A series of antibody agglutination tests indicated that she had an active infection of *F. tularensis*.

It turns out that the young hunter had been ill earlier in November. In fact, two days after he hunted rabbits, he went to the hospital, but no diagnosis could be determined. The hospital contacted him on November 26, 1985, when a link was made between him and the woman. He was started on streptomycin treatment, which promptly resolved his health complaints. His blood tests, taken one week apart starting November 29, indicated active infection with *F. tularensis*. The woman's husband was tested as well starting December 3 and, after two weeks, showed a positive result for active *F. tularensis* infection. Bone marrow from both rabbits was tested at a CDC laboratory and *F. tularensis* was recovered.

ANIMAL SOURCES OF INFECTION

F. tularensis is widely distributed in natural settings in the United States and other countries in the northern hemisphere. Over 100 animal species can be infected with *F. tularensis*. Small animals in the wild—particularly infected rabbits, field voles, squirrels, field mice, and wetland animals like the beaver and muskrat—are sources of *F. tularensis* when humans handle them. Veterinarians are exposed from handling infected domestic cats. Even domestic dogs, as previously noted (Chapter 3), have been instrumental in the transmission of tularemia to humans.

Muskrats are popular small game for trappers. They resemble beavers and are found in wetlands like marshes or rivers. Muskrats are reservoirs of *F. tularensis* and have been responsible for outbreaks in hunters, trappers, and furriers. *F. tularensis* type B, the less virulent form, has caused tularemia in muskrat trappers. An epidemic of tularemia in Vermont trappers in 1968 caused 47 cases associated with handling muskrats (Figure 6.1) within 4 weeks of exposure.[2]

RABBIT FEVER

The long history of infected wild rabbits has given tularemia the common name "rabbit fever." Contact between hunters and infected rabbits reflected 90% of tularemia cases in the United States before 1944. Cottontail rabbits, marsh hares, and swamp rabbits are common reservoirs of infection. When skinning or dressing rabbits, hunters are exposed to infected carcasses, rabbit blood, and other body substances. In the 1960s, it was estimated that between 6% and 17% of trappers and North American natives were positive for anti-tularense antibodies, evidence of a previous exposure to *F. tularensis*.

The processing and skinning of rabbit carcasses by trappers is a well-established source of human infection with *F. tularensis*. *F. tularensis* can survive in frozen rabbit meat for months, but the bacterium is inactivated by high heat. Therefore, eating inadequately cooked rabbits can also cause tularemia.

Figure 6.1 Muskrats (shown here) and other wetland animals are known reservoirs of *F. tularensis* type B.

ARTHROPOD BITES

The primary vectors of *F. tularensis* are ticks in the United States, former Soviet Union, and Japan; mosquitoes in the former Soviet Union, Scandinavia, and the Baltic region; and biting flies in Utah, Nevada, and California in the United States, as well as in the former Soviet Union. The tick is the most significant vector and reservoir of *F. tularensis* in the United States (Table 6.1).

Table 6.1 Ticks of Tularemia in the United States

Tick	Species	Location in the United States
Lone Star	*Amblyomma americanum*	Southern ⅓ of U.S.
Rocky Mountain Wood	*Dermacentor andersoni*	Western Mountains
Pacific Coast	*Dermacentor occidentalis*	West Coast
American Dog	*Dermacentor variabilis*	Eastern ½ of U.S. West Coast

Source: Drummond, Roger. *Ticks and What You Can Do About Them*. Berkeley, CA: Wilderness Press, 1990.

Both **transstadial** and **transovarial** transmission of *F. tularensis* can occur with ticks. Transstadial transmission occurs when one immature stage acquires the infectious agent while feeding and then maintains the infection through the next molt and transfers it to a new host the next time it feeds. Transovarial transmission occurs when the female tick acquires the infection while feeding and then transfers *F. tularensis* to the developing ova. The newly hatched larvae are infectious without having taken a blood meal.

PREVENTING TICK-BORNE TULAREMIA

Ticks detect their host by sensing carbon dioxide. Ticks feed on animals infected with *F. tularensis* and then transmit the bacterium into humans by latching on and biting the skin. A harpoon-like mouthpart called a hypostome pushes into the skin, and barbs (found under the hypostome) anchor the tick and make it hard to pull out.[3] The teeth draw blood, which the tick sucks up, thereby increasing its size 25- to 50-fold (Figure 6.2).

Preventing transmission relies on using personal protective measures. To identify ticks readily, one should wear light-colored clothing when out in long grass or in a wooded forest. Clothes covered in ticks should be laundered immediately when returning home. People

THE INVENTION OF DEET

The Agricultural Research Service (ARS) of the United States Department of Agriculture (USDA) is the research agency mandated to protect crops and livestock from pests and disease, improve the quality and safety of agricultural products, research how to sustain soil, and ensure profitability for farmers. The ARS had a $1 billion budget in 2003 and employs 2,100 scientists and 6,000 other employees at 100 research locations in the United States.

The ARS discovered DEET in the 1950s amongst thousands of substances tested to repel mosquitoes (See figure). In tests conducted by the United States Army and Air Force, DEET was combined with permethrin on military uniforms and was found to be 99.9% protective against mosquitoes even after two detergent washings of the uniforms.

With the discovery of Lyme disease and its vector (the deer tick), agricultural scientists showed that skin sprayed with a 30% concentration of DEET was an effective barrier to deer ticks. DEET alone was found to be over 80% effective against ticks and 97% against mosquitoes. Approximately 230 products containing DEET are licensed and approved for use by the United States Environmental Protection Agency (EPA).

should prepare for going outdoors by wearing long-sleeved shirts tucked into the pants at the waist and pants tucked into socks at the ankles. DEET repellent should be applied to the skin (30% concentration) and 0.5% permethrin spray onto clothing.

The American Academy of Pediatrics (AAP) makes recommendations on children's medical health. The AAP advises against the use of DEET on children younger than two months of age. Additionally, the AAP recommends against applying DEET to children's hands because of their tendency to lick

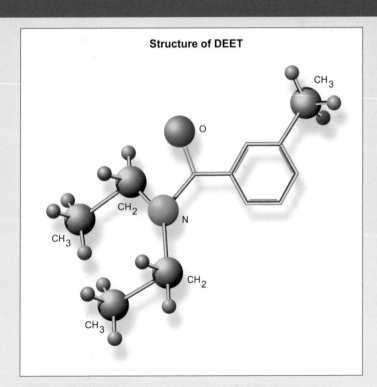

Structure of DEET

DEET is an insecticide used to prevent **tick-borne** tularemia. DEET has been found 80% effective against ticks and is found in numerous repellants.

Figure 6.2 Ticks feed on animals infected with *F. tularemia* and then transmit it to humans by biting the skin. On the left is an adult tick, while on the right is an engorged adult tick following a blood meal.

their fingers. The AAP also recommends that DEET be washed off children when they return back indoors.

Removal of ticks should be done very carefully. As it takes days for the tick to infect a person with bacterial pathogens, one can take the time to remove the tick using tweezers so as to not crush the tick. Tearing apart, crushing, or otherwise leaving the tick behind in one's skin can allow the tick's mouthparts to cause infection. Using tweezers and pulling steadily removes the whole tick. Not only should the skin lesion be disinfected with alcohol, but the excised tick should be killed in alcohol and flushed down the toilet.

7

Three Occupational Exposure Case Studies

LABORATORY-ACQUIRED TULAREMIA

In May 2004, two Boston University researchers became ill while working to develop a tularemia vaccine. The researchers were using a modified strain of *F. tularensis* sent to them from the University of Nebraska in Lincoln.[1] In September 2004, a third researcher became ill. Once tularemia was suspected, the vial of modified *F. tularensis* was analyzed. The CDC laboratory at Fort Collins, Colorado confirmed that the vial shipped from Nebraska to Boston University contained virulent *F. tularensis* type A in addition to the modified strain intended for research purposes.

Investigators suspect that the modified strain was contaminated and that it was responsible for the exposure and, subsequently, the researchers' infection. Blood used to promote the growth of bacterial stock had come from rabbits on a South Carolina farm. Investigators hypothesized that the material shipped to Boston that was supposed to be non-virulent had been contaminated by rabbit blood that harbored infectious *F. tularensis* type A, the most virulent form of tularemia infection for humans.

The exposure of these three university researchers highlights that "rabbit fever" is still a significant naturally-occurring infection in the United States. Confirming a case of active tularemia infection involves establishing laboratory proof of rising antibody in titration between two separate tests conducted 10 to 14 days apart.

Occupational exposures underscore the need for health and safety measures to prevent human exposure to sources of tularemia. Laboratory worker absences for illness can be indicators of laboratory exposure to infectious material. After tularemia is suspected, an examination of the worker's symptoms of fever (an early sign of tularemia) is performed to identify linked cases. Infection control specialists and well-trained workplace health and safety committees are both essential to establishing safety in laboratory research settings. Knowledge of the potential infectivity of biological materials used in experimentation is also essential. A vaccination against tularemia is used for laboratory researchers in regular contact with *F. tularensis*, but the development of a safe vaccine for wider dissemination is a current goal of the U.S. Department of Health and Human Services (HHS).

Laboratory Safety

Typhoidal tularemia has such a high virulence that strict laboratory precautions must be taken in handling material that includes *F. tularensis* type A. Whereas a few thousand *Bacillus anthracis* bacteria are required to cause anthrax, the inhalation of just 10 *F. tularensis* type A bacteria can kill if the infection is left untreated. Therefore, laboratory personnel should be alerted to the possibility that tularemia is clinically suspected before laboratory work begins, so that appropriate precautions can be implemented.

In the clinical laboratories to which doctors refer their patients for tests, only routine diagnostic procedures are available. Sometimes at this stage, it is not known what pathogen the patients are infected with. At these U.S. government-rated Level A laboratories, the range of protocols employed are usually limited to Gram stains, spot tests, and motility tests (Figure 7.1). If tularemia is suspected, patient samples are sent to Level B laboratories that have the ability to isolate and confirm *F. tularensis*, and laboratory personnel are notified in advance of their risk of exposure. Level B laboratories are usually state public health laboratories in which Biological Safety Level-2 (BSL-2) conditions are in effect (*e.g.*, using biosafety cabinets to prevent exposure to biological hazards).

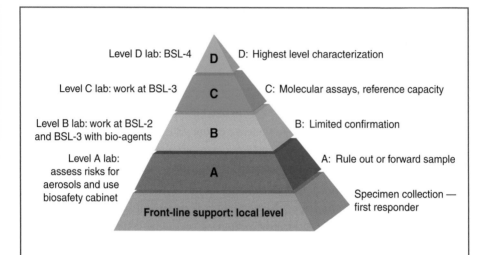

Level D lab: BSL-4   **D**   D: Highest level characterization

Level C lab: work at BSL-3   **C**   C: Molecular assays, reference capacity

Level B lab: work at BSL-2 and BSL-3 with bio-agents   **B**   B: Limited confirmation

Level A lab: assess risks for aerosols and use biosafety cabinet   **A**   A: Rule out or forward sample

Front-line support: local level   Specimen collection — first responder

Figure 7.1 Diagnostic laboratories in the United States are organized by the Centers for Disease Control and Prevention according to the level of safety precautions. In case of an outbreak, local, front-line labs and Level A facilities rule out organisms or send samples to the next level for further testing. Level B labs can identify organisms such as anthrax or plague. *F. tularensis* is confirmed at Level C facilities. The most dangerous types of organisms, such as smallpox, are sent to Level D labs.

Given the high risk of *F. tularensis* infection to Level B laboratory scientists, personal protective equipment (including face masks, eye protection, surgical gloves, protective gowns, and shoe covers) is worn to decrease occupational exposure (Figure 7.2). Attention to avoiding spills or splashes becomes paramount for workers who directly handle *F. tularensis* samples. When *F. tularensis* type A is suspected, biological samples like patient tissues or fluids must be sent for testing to a higher safety level laboratory with BSL-3 conditions. Also, if manipulation of the infected tissues or fluids necessitates grinding, centrifuging (spinning), shaking, or animal studies, these investigations are required to be done in BSL-3 facilities. The potential for occupational exposure from aerosols is high;

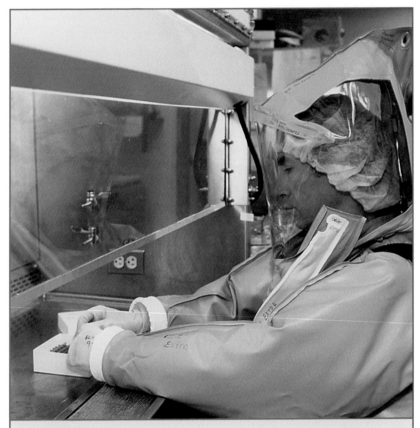

Figure 7.2 Because of the high risk of *F. tularensis* infections, laboratory scientists wear personal protective equipment and work under a flow hood to prevent the spread of the disease organism.

therefore, an isolated zone with a dedicated air system, exhaust, and decontamination is required.

Infection Control

Infection control practices in hospital settings involve adherence to routine gown, glove, and masking protocols to prevent exposure of any body substances to infected patients. Person-to-person transmission between tularemia patients and others is not a concern; therefore, infection control practices in medical settings need not include patient isolation. Routine body substance precautions for hospitals are sufficient. Infectious patient laundry and clothing is bagged and laundered at high temperature to kill bacteria.

The handling of deceased persons requires significant care to prevent occupational exposure to infectious body substances, with particular emphasis on reducing the aerosolization of particles. Postmortem care involves Standard Universal Precautions in a surgical scrub suite with personnel dressed in cap, gown, protective goggles, shoe coverings, and double pairs of surgical gloves with an interposed layer of cut-proof synthetic mesh. Autopsy procedures require workers to wear respirators and avoid bone sawing, for instance. Embalming of cadavers that contain *F. tularensis* is strongly discouraged.

LAWNMOWER TULAREMIA

At Martha's Vineyard, Massachusetts in the summer of 2000, a 43-year-old man became ill one week after mowing his lawn. Unbeknownst to him, he was suffering from infection with *F. tularensis* type A, the rare but much more virulent form of tularemia that causes pneumonia when inhaled. His delay in seeking medical treatment may have contributed to his death.[2] Another man soon became ill after coming into contact with a dead rabbit while cutting brush on his property. He too had pneumonia and later was confirmed to have tularemia. Two others reported seeing a dead rabbit close to where they were gardening within two weeks prior to their tularemia infections. Local health officials recognized 15 cases of tularemia in the Martha's Vineyard outbreak between May and October in 2000, 11 cases of which were confirmed to be *F. tularensis* type A pneumonic tularemia.

All but one of the people infected in the 2000 outbreak were men and half were professional landscapers. Public health researchers recalled that, in an earlier 1978 outbreak, two of the eight cases were gardeners. The researchers realized a possible occupational risk for gardeners and landscapers on Martha's Vineyard.

In the 1930s, gaming and hunting clubs in Martha's Vineyard imported nearly 25,000 cottontail rabbits from Oklahoma, Missouri, and Arkansas—states in which *F. tularensis* was endemic. Thus, "rabbit fever" cases have been reported annually in the residents of Massachusetts from the 1930s to the present day. In fact, the only two modern outbreaks of naturally acquired primary pneumonic tularemia in all the United States have occurred on Martha's Vineyard, in 1978 and in 2000.

The Aerosolized Agent

Dr. Katherine Feldman and a group of researchers evaluated whether the act of lawn-mowing could aerosolize *F. tularensis* bacteria, which they assumed was being inhaled by landscapers. Their serological study in 2001 compared blood samples from Martha's Vineyard landscapers to that of controls to see how many in the landscaping profession had been exposed to *F. tularensis*.[3] Out of a group of 132 landscapers, 12 (9%) were positive for anti-tularense antibodies versus only one person in a large control group of non-landscaping residents of Martha's Vineyard.

Dr. Feldman's study found that landscapers were nine times more likely to have anti-tularense antibodies in their blood than people in the control population. Within the group of landscapers who used power leaf blowers, 15% were positive for antibodies versus just 2% for landscapers who did not use power blowers. Power blowing was significantly associated with landscapers who developed tularemia infection.

In the tularemia research community, the phrase "lawn-mower tularemia" had already been coined by 1990 when Drs. McCarthy and Murphy of the Department of Pediatrics, at the University of Tennessee Medical Center in Knoxville identified an unusual exposure to a rabbit (the only risk factor)

(continued on page 76)

OBSERVATIONAL EPIDEMIOLOGY

Epidemiology is the study of diseases and other health conditions that affect human populations: their causes, their control, and the factors that determine their distribution in communities. One way that epidemiologists conduct research is by observational study.

Epidemiologists research what factors (*e.g.*, behaviors, exposures, location of worker residence) may be associated with confirmed cases of a disease under investigation. Factors potentially associated with a diseased group of persons are compared to a matched control group of persons who do not have the disease in order to identify and measure any difference between the groups. The relative risk is the calculation of the ratio of the risk of disease among the exposed individuals to the risk in the unexposed individuals. This type of research is called the case-control study. The observational data is organized into a 2x2 contingency table (below):

Case-Control Study		
	DISEASE (CASES)	NO DISEASE (CONTROLS)
Exposed	a	b
Unexposed	c	d

If the controls are adequately matched with the cases for all other possible factors, and if the frequency of the disease under study in the population is small, the relative risk can be approximated using a mathematical ratio derived from the values in the contingency table. The ratio *ad/bc* represents the cross-product ratio and is called the odds ratio. It expresses the statistical strength of an association between the exposure to a particular factor and the disease.

In the case-control study of the year 2000 tularemia outbreak on Martha's Vineyard reported by Dr. Feldman and colleagues, the 2x2 contingency table would be:

Tularemia on Martha's Vineyard, 2000

	TULAREMIA (CASES)	NO TULAREMIA (CONTROLS)
Used a lawn mower or brush cutter two weeks before illness (Exposed)	8	30
No lawn mowing (Unexposed)	2	69

The odds ratio is *ad/bc* or (8x69)/(30x2) = 9.2. This suggests that there was over 9 times greater risk of getting tularemia when cutting the lawn than if not doing landscaping in Martha's Vineyard at the time of the outbreak.

Sources:

Lilienfeld, David E., and Paul D. Stolley. *Foundations of Epidemiology*, Third Edition. New York, NY: Oxford University Press, 1994.

Feldman, K. A., R. E. Enscore, S. L. Lathrop, et al. "An Outbreak of Primary Pulmonary Tularemia on Martha's Vineyard." *New England Journal of Medicine* 345(22)(2001): 1601–1606.

(continued from page 73)

in two sick adolescent boys.[4] The 13-year-old boy had experienced daily fevers, cough, and swollen lymph nodes for over 36 days before a test for anti-tularense antibodies was positive. His friend also tested positive for anti-tularense antibodies. The pediatricians sought to discover the direct exposure expected of this **zoonotic** infection. After much perseverance, the pediatricians were able to get a reluctant admission that the boys had run over a rabbit (twice) while mowing the lawn. Adolescent fear of repercussion in particular was a strong factor in the youths not readily offering their exposure history to their doctors. Patients do not easily recall, nor treat with significance, any direct risk to their health presented by lawn mowing over animal carcasses.

Preventing Landscaping Exposure

Public health officials have warned landscapers on Martha's Vineyard to wear dust masks to prevent inhaling tularemia bacteria stirred up by mowing or blowing. Despite the warnings, landscapers were quoted in the Vineyard Gazette as saying that the masks are too hot to wear.[5] However, a survey of mask protection undertaken by Feldman and colleagues noted a large increase in awareness and mask-wearing after the 2000 pneumonic tularemia outbreak. Ninety-two percent of landscapers reported never wearing a mask prior to 2000, but, after the outbreak, landscapers who claimed to never wear a mask dropped to 58%. Public health officials are hoping that the message will spread and ultimately block the respiratory route of tularemia transmission in this area (Table 7.1).

The research at Martha's Vineyard targeted the occupational exposure of landscapers, but these findings are applicable to all gardeners in tularemia-endemic areas. Mowing is a process of mechanical propellant that does not discriminate between professional or personal mowing; for example, Martha's Vineyard landscapers reported mowing their own lawns, not just the property of clients, before coming down

Table 7.1 Preventing Landscaping Exposure to *F. tularensis.*

Wear dust face masks.
Survey the property prior to landscaping to chase off animals.
Remove animal carcasses before landscaping.
Take care in disposing of animal feces found on the grounds.
Use properly attached lawn mower collection bags.
Use properly attached leaf blower collection bags.

with tularemia. Medical professionals need to be aware that a febrile illness after lawn-mowing in a tularemia-endemic area can be indicative of *F. tularensis* infection. With death rates of 30% to 60% before the advent of antibiotics and 5% to 9% since, prompt evaluation, identification, and treatment of pneumonic tularemia could mean the difference between life and death.

THRESHING HAY

In a retrospective analysis of 123 tularemia cases in Finland from the year 1982, 53 cases, mainly from Oulu, were found to be typhoidal tularemia with no reported portal of entry.[6] Of these typhoidal tularemia patients, 44 were farmers or from farm families who worked the land prior to the onset of illness. All cases had fever and fatigue, and over three-quarters reported respiratory symptoms. The common link between the farmers who became ill was a report of having recently cut fresh hay in the fields or baling, threshing, or handling new straw on the farm.

Swedish researchers also drew a link between farmers who had been exposed in August of 2000 to hay that contained vole dung. This differed from the Finland outbreak associated with freshly cut hay. In the Swedish epidemic, farmers recalled seeing mounds made by voles throughout their hay fields, which they eventually drove over during the hay harvest. The farmers in the Swedish outbreak became ill with typhoidal tularemia from aerosolized *F. tularensis* present in the vole dung that was in the stored hay bales they were moving in the barns.[7] The survival time of *F. tularensis* in straw was studied in Russia in 1953.[8] It was shown to survive 671 days and still be able to produce viable cultures and disease in mice. The Swedish outbreak resulted from hay that had been harvested and stored over the previous winter, and that was just being moved by farmers during the summer of 2000.

Overall, Scandinavian countries have the next highest incidence of human tularemia outside the United States. In tularemia-endemic areas, the small animal populations pose a clear risk to farmers who cultivate and move hay. Pneumonic tularemia may occur without the overt symptoms (*i.e.*, ulcers or lymphadenitis) that normally provide the doctor clues towards a diagnosis of tularemia.

8

Francisella tularensis: A Biological Weapon

BIOLOGICAL WARFARE

Biological warfare has a long and disturbing history. Research into large-scale biological warfare has been done by governments with the means and resources capable of building and maintaining costly and complex military infrastructures. Biological weapons development comprises production of the agent, stabilization (often by freeze drying), and production of the dispersal method (usually spray devices or cluster bombs). The most destructive effect on populations throughout history has been from disease, more so than conventional weapons used in war, so it followed that warring nations would try harnessing biological agents as weapons. Bioweapons designed to inflict tularemia have been developed by several countries, especially during the Second World War: Japan, the former Soviet Union, and the United States have each at different points in history stockpiled *F. tularensis* for offensive weapons.

JAPANESE UNIT 731

Defense programs against biological warfare are now commonplace and publicly discussed, but back in the 1930s and 1940s offensive biological weapons were being developed in secret and tested on thousands of people. In the 1930s, thousands of Chinese people were rumored to have been killed from biological attacks by the Japanese Army in eastern Asia. Biological warfare research facilities existed in Beijing, Shanghai, Canton, Hailar, Singapore, Rangoon, and Bangkok.[1] The governments of the Soviet Union and the United States thought they were just rumors.

After the capture of Japanese Army scientists in Manchuria by Soviet troops, and during the U.S. occupation of Japan after World War II, it became clear that biological experimentation on many thousands of Chinese citizens, Soviet people, and prisoners of war had been a long-standing program of the wartime Japanese government. It was significant and widespread, killing 10,000 persons between 1932 and 1945, even though most world leaders had agreed in principle to ban biological warfare with the 1925 Geneva Protocol.

The Japanese government had expansionist interests into eastern Asia before and during World War II. In Japanese-occupied Manchuria, Shiro Ishii was the Commander of the biological warfare Unit 731, which was disguised as the Water Purification Unit of the occupying Kwantung Army. Commander Ishii (a physician) wanted to prove his ideas that biological weapons were an efficient means for undertaking warfare and preferred the unethical practice of human experimentation for direct proof. Unit 731 received 200,000 yen in government funding and 300 staff members in an initial start-up phase in 1932.

Unit 731 and other units of the Japanese Army studied the effects on humans of many diseases including plague, typhus, smallpox, yellow fever, hepatitis, gangrene, encephalitis, whooping cough, diphtheria, typhoid fever, meningitis, tuberculosis, salmonella, and tularemia. Japanese army medical commanders perfected weapons to drop plague-infected fleas from airplanes onto cities, contaminate community water supplies, release infected animals into Soviet herds, and lace food with *B. anthracis*, *Vibrio cholerae*, *Shigella*, *Salmonella*, and *Yersinia pestis*. These unethical practices came to light in the testimony of Japanese scientists captured by both the Soviet military and the occupying U.S. military.

SOVIET UNION BIOPREPARAT

Following World War II, mass vaccinations against *F. tularensis* for citizens and workers in tularemia-endemic areas were done by the Soviet government. At the same time, a Soviet program to research biological pathogens for biowarfare began. By the 1950s, military biological production facilities were in operation across the country, even within several town centers. This proximity affected Sverdlovsk, Russia on April 1979 when a breach of containment of bacteria in the local plant occurred, contaminating citizens in the surrounding community. The breach led to an airborne leak of anthrax spores that killed nearly 100 citizens living downwind.[2] The leak had been caused by workers at the military biological production facility who forgot to replace a filter in an exhaust system. It purportedly took five years to clean up. The event called into question the validity of the Soviet agreement to the 1972 Biological Arms Convention.

Biopreparat was the Soviet state-sponsored pharmaceutical agency whose primary goal was to produce biological weapons from pathogenic agents. Forty sites in Russia and Kazakhstan comprised the massive research and production work. The biological research laboratories employed 55,000 workers during the 1970s and 1980s. Even up to the 1990s and beyond, the bioweapons production of several pathogens continued. The Soviets were able to engineer *F. tularensis* strains that were resistant to antibiotics and strains that were not amenable to vaccine protection. In 1979, Dr. Ken Alibek began work to weaponize *F. tularensis.* Bombs filled with vaccine-resistant strains of *F. tularensis* were tested on Rebirth Island in the summer of 1982. Five hundred monkeys that had been immunized against *F. tularensis* using the conventional vaccine were subjected to the bombings and nearly all of them died from the engineered *F. tularensis.*

UNITED STATES "EIGHT BALL"

After learning of the biowarfare research done in Japan, fears grew that other nations were also building bioweapons. In 1942, the United States began a biological research defense program to protect food and water

BATTLE OF STALINGRAD

Between September 1942 and February 1943, the German Army marched through Russia in the battle to take over Stalingrad in WWII. Tularemia, however, was believed to overpower the German soldiers in the end. History shows that, in times of the great wars, disease and pestilence caused the most significant loss of life. The indiscriminate efficiency with which disease annihilated populations gave military leaders the idea to experiment with germ warfare and biological weapons.

Dr. Ken Alibek, first deputy chief of the Soviet Biopreparat Program from 1988 to 1992, has publicly said that tularemia was in fact used as a bioweapon by the Soviet army against German troops outside Stalingrad in late 1942 (See figure). In the year previous to the German invasion, the Soviet Union had 10,000 cases of tularemia. At the height of the battle, there were over 100,000 but this number returned to 10,000 in 1943.

Alibek reported that 70% of those infected came down with pneumonic tularemia, suggesting intentional aerosolized dissemination. Citizens in the surrounding regions came down with the disease a week after the first German troop outbreak. It is thought that a shift in the wind direction or spread via rodents caused the tularemia exposure to the surrounding communities. Given the catastrophic troop loss, the Commander of the German Sixth Army surrendered the remaining 91,000 troops on February 2, 1943.

Source: Alibek, K. *BioHazard*. New York, NY: Dell Publishing, 1999.

supplies. By 1944, research on offensive bioweapons was also under way.

During and after World War II, members of the Seventh-day Adventist church objected to military service but instead volunteered, at Walter Reed Medical Center and also at Fort

Dr. Ken Alibek, Distinguished Professor at George Mason University in Virginia, is the former First Deputy Chief of the Soviet Union's offensive biological weapons program.

Detrick, Maryland, to undergo biological experimentation in a program called Operation Whitecoat.[3] The United States Army used a one million-liter hollow metal sphere, called the "Eight Ball," to administer biological aerosols in order to evaluate vaccine effectiveness (Figure 8.1). Between 1954 and 1973, volunteers were placed in the Eight Ball and exposed to *F. tularensis* and Q fever, among other agents. The service of the Adventists and other volunteers led to the realization that antibiotics could be used to cure weaponized Q fever and tularemia.

By the late 1960s, the U.S. military had stockpiles of biological agents that were in weaponized form. But the world position on biological warfare turned once again to rejecting that approach and Warsaw Pact nations developed a biological disarmament proposal at the Convention on the Prohibition of the Development, Production, and Stockpiling of Bacteriological and Toxic Weapons and Their Destruction, ratified April 1972 and effective March 1975. Under this disarmament protocol, The United Nations Security Council would evaluate lodged complaints about breaches to the biological weapons convention and could undertake inspections of countries' weapons facilities. The United States offensive bioweapons program was dismantled, and stockpiles were destroyed in 1969 and 1970 by order of President Nixon.

OUTBREAK OR BIOLOGICAL ATTACK?

After the New York City and Pentagon attacks of September 11, 2001, it became clear that there are groups intent on destroying the way of life of citizens of the United States using any means at their disposal. Terrorist use of biowarfare agents has become a grave concern. Indeed, intentional biological contamination of the public is not unknown within the United States. In 1984, the Rajneeshee cult intentionally spread *Salmonella typhimurium* around The Dalles, Oregon to sicken citizens and thus prevent them from voting in an upcoming election.[4] On August 29 of that year, the Rajneeshees began sprinkling

Figure 8.1 During the 1950s and 1960s, U.S. Army scientists experimented with biological warfare agents. Volunteers were placed into the giant stainless steel "Eight Ball" and exposed to biological aerosols, including *F. tularensis*. The scientists concluded that weaponized tularemia could be treated with antibiotics.

S. typhimurium in personal drinking glasses, on doorknobs and urinal handles, on produce at the local supermarket, and on salad bars in 11 restaurants. Their covert actions caused 750 cases of food poisoning, 45 of which required hospitalization. Despite an epidemiological investigation, suspicions of an intentional attack were only substantiated after a police investigation resulted in one of the cult members admitting the attack one year later. Investigators assumed that, if this was an intentional contamination, some group would have called the media or authorities to claim responsibility, reporting:

> We assumed that if the motive was either extortion or terrorism, a public statement would have been issued to intimidate or create widespread fear. In fact, the incident was planned as a covert tactical strike.

It is a fallacy to assume that an intentional contamination with biological agents can be clearly distinguished from a rare, random outbreak at first report. It is likely that authorities would be completely in the dark as to the activities of terrorists at work to undermine the safety of innocent citizens. The most that can be done is to prepare for the possibility of biological terrorism by gathering all available knowledge and incorporating it into epidemiologic surveillance and investigation strategies. Notifying law enforcement of a possible biological attack is now also a primary consideration in an outbreak investigation.

F. tularensis is thought to be one probable agent that terrorists would consider because it can be aerosolized and also because it can be lethal if untreated. For this reason, *F. tularensis* is a Category A agent (see Chapter 4), which means that the U.S. government recognizes the grave potential of tularemia as a biological terror. The tularemia bacterium is easy to disseminate, causes high mortality, will cause public panic, and thus requires diligent preparedness, including enhanced disease surveillance and terrorism drills. Other Category A agents include the pathogens that cause smallpox, plague, anthrax, hemorrhagic fever, and botulism. In comparison to inhalational plague or anthrax, tularemia is predicted to have a lower **case fatality rate** and slower progression of illness.

It is difficult to distinguish between an outbreak of community-acquired pneumonia and an outbreak of tularemia arising from an intentional biological contamination. Table 8.1

Table 8.1 Tularemia-specific Warning Signs of Intentional Biological Contamination

Characteristics	Natural Outbreak	Intentional Biological Contamination
Nature of tularemia	Zoonotic disease requires a zoonotic reservoir.	No zoonotic reservoir (*e.g.*, cases in an urban setting).
Epidemic curve	Seasonal distribution related to occupation (landscaping, farming) or sporadic laboratory-acquired cases.	Point source epidemic (attributed to one building) or a set of point source attacks (a set of sites).
Incubation period	3–5 days average.	Shorter incubation period (involving a unique strain or higher concentration of inoculum).
Population at risk	Inhalational tularemia is rare. Groups affected tend to be in a similar occupational class.	Large numbers of disparate citizens affected (assisted via aerosolization).
Case fatality rate	Morbidity and mortality are predictable.	Higher mortality (higher concentration of inoculum, possible use of antibiotic resistant strain).

summarizes the issues regarding epidemic inhalational tularemia, comparing a natural outbreak to an intentional presentation.

Cases of inhalational tularemia are rare despite the outbreaks that have occurred in Massachusetts on Martha's Vineyard (see Chapter 7). The accepted profile of an inhalational tularemia patient is the landscaper, farmer, or person working the land who accidentally aerosolizes *F. tularensis* that is already present from an animal source in the area. Laboratory-acquired cases of tularemia also occur (see Chapter 7). These are risks that are known and somewhat preventable. In contrast, a biological attack with *F. tularensis* would be one that catches the public off-guard. Features of such an artificial outbreak would contrast with the rare nature of tularemia and its normal association with rural activities. One example is the likely occurrence of the vast majority of cases all at once and likely in one location. The persons affected would not have obvious connections to an animal vector. The sudden appearance of patients at primary care physicians' offices and a surge in calls to 911 regarding respiratory distress would also be distinguishing characteristics of an intentional *F. tularensis* dissemination.[5]

Notifying law enforcement of a possible biological terrorist attack should occur as soon as epidemiologists suspect an intentional or unexplainable aerosol, food, or water transmission in an outbreak, or a definitively confirmed case of uncommon disease or illness with a genetically altered organism. However, an immediate call to the Federal Bureau of Investigation should occur after notification by a group or individual that a terrorist attack is under way or will occur, a dispersal device is discovered, or powder is sent inside a letter.[6]

THE MISSED SENTINEL CASE

A 2003 report of the Martha's Vineyard tularemia outbreak that occurred in 2000 described a missed sentinel case—a Connecticut resident who was not initially diagnosed with tularemia.[7] Originally, his symptoms were nondescript: diarrheal illness, right-sided head and neck pain, fever, persistent anorexia, and severe weight loss that resulted in the loss of 20 pounds in just 5 days starting May 29, 2000. He did not seek medical care for the first week after onset of symptoms. After seeing his physician, he received clarithromycin for 10 days for bronchopneumonia after right middle-lobe infiltrate was discovered on his chest X-ray and he developed a fever of 103° F. His illness was confirmed as tularemia only after he made an inquiry in August 2000 after seeing publicity about the tularemia outbreak near his cottage at Martha's Vineyard, prompting him to have his blood tested by a Connecticut private lab. The actual outbreak on Martha's Vineyard was detected by local hospital clinical staff knowledgable about pneumonic tularemia as a summer illness.

Each case of inhalational tularemia should be investigated as a **sentinel event**. Local hospitals, laboratories, and health care providers report suspected cases to public health officials as required by state notifiable disease surveillance guidelines. State cases are reported to the National Notifiable Disease Surveillance System (NNDSS) of the CDC, where case data is reviewed for trends in geographic, demographic, and seasonal distribution. The cases are compared to expected patterns that are based on amassed historical epidemiologic trends.

Respiratory secretions and blood samples collected from patients are sent to a laboratory that is aware of the risks of *F. tularensis* exposure. The need for laboratory containment and safe handling procedures is paramount to avoid laboratory-acquired infection (see Chapter 7). A rapid diagnostic procedure by a National Public Health Laboratory Network group, involving microscopic detection of *F. tularensis* using fluorescent-labeled antibodies, can provide a quick presumptive diagnosis. From a respiratory sample (sputum or pharyngeal wash), *F. tularensis* can be grown in culture for a confirmatory diagnosis.

ECONOMIC IMPACT OF A BIOLOGICAL ATTACK

In 1969, the World Health Organization (WHO) studied the health aspects of a hypothetical biological attack: a 50-kg drop of virulent aerosolized *F. tularensis* over a city of five million people. The WHO predicted that such an attack would cause 250,000 serious casualties, including 19,000 deaths. Illness would take hold for several weeks and perhaps even months.

The economic impact of inhalation tularemia from such a biological attack would be significant. Loss of life, costs per day of hospital admission, outpatient treatment, laboratory costs, and pharmaceutical costs are some of the items that were factored into a 1997 CDC model.[8] The cost per 100,000 persons exposed to an attack using anthrax, *F. tularensis,* or brucellosis was predicted as shown in Table 8.2.

Table 8.2 Costs of a Biological Attack

Biological Attack	Cost per 100,000 Persons Exposed (Billion dollars)
Anthrax	$18.1–26.2
Tularemia	$3.8–5.4
Brucellosis	$0.5–0.6

Source: Kaufmann, Meltzer, and Schmid. Emerging Infectious Diseases. April–June 1997.

Early identification and intervention were predicted by this study to be the best ways to reduce the human and financial impact of a biological attack. Attributing tularemia cases to natural outbreaks or intentional biological contamination will not change the planned mobilization of public health authorities to identify the cases, halt the spread, and ensure treatment for those affected by tularemia in the community.

9

Looking to the Future

TULAREMIA VACCINE

The U.S. National Institute of Allergy and Infectious Diseases (NIAID) is the government agency responsible for infectious disease research on pathogens of **bioterrorism**. Since anthrax was released through the U.S. postal system in the fall of 2001, a spotlight has shone brightly on the need to protect the U.S. population from intentional dissemination of biological agents. Bioterrorism is defined as intentional release of microorganisms or their toxins to harm people and generate widespread panic in society. Typhoidal tularemia causes 30% mortality if left untreated or 3% mortality if treated early and aggressively. The primary prevention strategy to avoid a large susceptible population from succumbing to tularemia is vaccination. A safe and effective vaccine to protect the population from *F. tularensis* infection is currently being sought by the NIAID.

After World War II, the former Soviet Union used a live **attenuated** (weakened) vaccine to protect millions of citizens living in enzootic areas (regions with constant tularemia in local animal populations). Previous Russian studies of avirulent vaccines (those made from non-living cellular components) showed that inactivated vaccines were unsuitable for developing protective antibodies and instead elicited allergic reactions.[1] In enzootic areas, over half of the Soviet population was affected by tularemia via infected rodent vectors, waterborne spread, and agricultural work leading to exposure to contaminated grain that aerosolized the *F. tularensis* bacterium. In 1957, a tularemia outbreak among 16 of 31 grain threshing farmers occurred in the Kostroma, Oblast region. Subsequent vaccination of 1,106 people in the immediate vicinity and 6,000 in the surrounding areas, combined with the cessation of threshing activities and the implementation of health education programs, resolved the outbreak. Vaccination was effective given that *F. tularensis* posed a high risk and subsequent sporadic cases only occurred in non-vaccinated persons.

The Foshay vaccine (*F. tularensis* killed by the chemical phenol) was developed by U.S. Army laboratory researchers working with the bacterium at Fort Detrick, Maryland from 1950 to 1959. In 1961, the Foshay vaccine was shown to provide no protection against respiratory exposure to *F. tularensis*. [2] The Foshay vaccine did not prevent local infection in humans, but could minimize the systemic infection of ulceroglandular tularemia.

In the 1950s, the U.S. Army also developed a live attenuated *F. tularensis* vaccine strain (LVS) from the live vaccine strain used in the Soviet Union. From 1960 to 1969, the new LVS vaccine was used to protect laboratory researchers. Laboratory-acquired tularemia cases at Fort Detrick, Maryland were compared between the Foshay vaccine period in the 1950s and the LVS vaccine period in the 1960s. [3] Cases of typhoidal tularemia decreased with the change to the new LVS vaccine, but no change in ulceroglandular tularemia was seen, just milder symptoms than when inoculated with the Foshay vaccine. Given this finding, the U.S. Working Group on Civilian Biodefense recommends that laboratory scientists who handle *F. tularensis* receive the LVS vaccine for their protection from occupational exposure. Protective immunity takes two weeks to develop and thus the LVS is not recommended for post-exposure treatment of persons already infected with *F. tularensis*.

REGIONAL CENTERS OF EXCELLENCE

Using a new decentralized organizational model, the U.S. Department of Health and Human Services (under its NIAID division) created Regional Centers of Excellence (RCEs) for Biodefense and Emerging Infectious Disease Research. Established in 2003, the institutions listed in Table 9.1 serve as hosts to eight RCEs.

These eight RCEs collaborate with several regional medical and university institutions in their vicinity. These centers facilitate training of researchers, build teams for emergency response, and initiate research projects. The centers are striving to develop a new tularemia vaccine, as well as new vaccines for anthrax, plague, smallpox, and Ebola. Through new

Table 9.1 Regional Centers of Excellence (RCE) for Biodefense and Emerging Infectious Disease Research

University of Chicago, Chicago, IL
Duke University, Durham, NC
Harvard University, Boston, MA
University of Maryland, College Park, MD
New York State Department of Health, Albany, NY
University of Texas Medical Branch, Galveston, TX
University of Washington, Seattle, WA
Washington University, St. Louis, MO

microbiology research, these centers are also developing innovative diagnostic tools. For example, Dr. Jeffrey Frelinger, Professor and Chair of Microbiology and Immunology at UNC-Chapel Hill, is using a $3.5 million research grant to develop a high throughput method to identify the precise molecules of the *F. tularensis* bacterium that are recognized by the human immune system.[4] Identifying and characterizing the molecules that activate the immune reaction will help facilitate the development of new vaccines and drugs against *F. tularensis* infection.

Dr. Thomas J. Inzana, Professor and Director of Clinical Microbiology at the Virginia-Maryland Regional College of Veterinary Medicine, was given $1 million to develop a vaccine diagnostic test for tularemia. Dr. Inzana will isolate and characterize the capsule-like substance on the surface of *F. tularensis* bacteria, as well as the outer membrane proteins that enable *F. tularensis* to survive inside human macrophages.[5] Dr. Inzana and his colleagues speculate that antibodies specific to the capsule will help clear bacteria not yet taken up by the macrophages and that T cells of the human immune system will kill macrophages that harbor the bacteria.

PHOTONIC BIOSENSOR

Dr. Inzana is also working with Dr. Kristie Cooper of Virginia Tech's Center for Photonic Technology (CPT) on a project to develop a photonic-based (optical) biosensor to detect *F. tularensis*. When placed in public places and on battlefields, the photonic biosensor will act as a rapid detector for aerosolized *F. tularensis* (Figure 9.1).[6]

The ultra-sensitive sensor under development is based on an optical fiber with a thin film that bears a one-molecule-thick coating of antibodies. When *F. tularensis* is present, bacterial antigens are bound by the antibodies, attaching bacteria to the coated fiber. When the bacteria attach, the change in evanescence (light that escapes through the fiber wall) is measured.

Tapping the air for early warning

The government has installed sensors in more than 30 cities, including San Diego, New York, and Washington, D.C. to monitor the air for deadly agents. The filters are checked regularly so that an attack would be detected prior to the onset of symptoms.

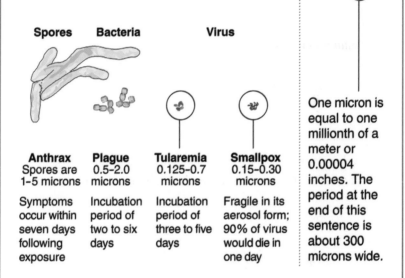

Spores	Bacteria	Virus	
Anthrax Spores are 1–5 microns	**Plague** 0.5–2.0 microns	**Tularemia** 0.125–0.7 microns	**Smallpox** 0.15–0.30 microns
Symptoms occur within seven days following exposure	Incubation period of two to six days	Incubation period of three to five days	Fragile in its aerosol form; 90% of virus would die in one day

One micron is equal to one millionth of a meter or 0.00004 inches. The period at the end of this sentence is about 300 microns wide.

SOURCES: American AirFilters; American Society of Heating, Refrigerating and Air-Conditioning Engineers Inc.; Centers for Disease Control and Prevention; Associated Press   **AP**

Figure 9.1 Early warning sensors help improve the response to possible bioterrorism emergencies.

Dr. Inzana is providing CPT with antibodies to the capsule (the outermost layer of the bacterium), which are thought to be better than antibodies to *F. tularensis* as a whole for avoiding cross-reactivity with similar antigens of other bacteria. The completed biosensor will be an innovative early warning system that provides security against intentional exposure to both military and civilian populations.

PUBLIC HEALTH PREPAREDNESS
AND RESPONSE DRILLS

To complement the above-mentioned innovations, health departments across the United States are conducting drills to evaluate local preparedness and response to bioterrorism emergencies. The state of Hawaii (among others) has used tularemia as its bioterrorism simulation exercise. One major objective of these exercises is to evaluate the local preparedness

U.S. STRATEGIC NATIONAL STOCKPILE–SNS

In 1999, the United States Congress directed the Department of Health and Human Services (HHS) and the Centers for Disease Control and Prevention (CDC) to establish a National Pharmaceutical Stockpile. The mandate of the National Pharmaceutical Stockpile was to be prepared to supply large quantities of essential medical material (antibiotics, chemical antidotes, antitoxins, life support medications, intravenous liquids, airway supplies, and other medical/surgical items) to affected areas in a national emergency within 12 hours. On March 1, 2003, the NPS became the Strategic National Stockpile (SNS) Program managed jointly by the Department of Homeland Security and HHS.

The SNS provides medical supplies free of charge and in sufficient quantities to assist and protect the citizens of several large cities. The function of the SNS is coordinated so that federal, state, and community resources can mobilize together to prepare and respond to a national disaster or terrorist action. If the biological agent is known during a natural or intentional outbreak, if for example tularemia is identified, then the affected state's governor's office will directly request deployment of SNS assets. The SNS also conducts nationwide preparedness training and educational programs that include teaching and anticipated requirements of the U.S. Strategic National Stockpile (SNS).

In the summer of 2004, the Hawaii Health Department had 210 employees play the roles of staff and patients in a mock tularemia attack. A bar-code system was tested to assist patients with follow-up services or medication refills.[7] Bar-code records were kept in a health department registry and each patient received a pocket card with the bar code and

state first responders to receive, secure, and distribute SNS assets. Critical to the success of this initiative is ensuring that capacity is developed at the federal, state, and local levels to receive, stage, and dispense SNS assets properly. The Technical Advisory Response Unit (TARU) members remain on-site to assist and advise state and local officials in putting the SNS assets to prompt and effective use.

In the event that the national emergency is broader in scope than one specific cause or outbreak, the SNS deploys Push Packages that contain pharmaceuticals, antidotes, and medical supplies for general health emergencies. Push Packages are already strategically located in secure warehouses across the United States and are ready for immediate deployment and arrival on-site within 12 hours of federal release. During the anthrax contamination in Washington, D.C. in the fall of 2001, HHS Secretary Tommy Thompson had available eight Push Packages, each containing 50 tons of pharmaceutical supplies and other medical supplies that could have provided enough ciprofloxacin and other antibiotics to treat two million Americans for 60 days.

Source: Center for Disease Control and Prevention. January 20, 2005. http://www.bt.cdc.gov/stockpile/

Figure 9.2 Biological terrorism simulation drills prepare first responders for intentional contamination scenarios involving any kind of biological or chemical attack. Personal protective gear is worn to prevent hazardous biological or chemical exposures.

contact phone numbers to access additional resources. The mock attack tested for ways to improve the distribution of medicine in a large-scale emergency.

The Knox County Health Department in Tennessee conducted a tularemia drill in August 2004 in which the simulation involved thousands of people being exposed to *F. tularensis*. Designed to evaluate the distribution of antibiotics from the SNS, the exercise required health responders to conduct triage, determine symptoms specific to tularemia (versus other symptoms issued in the mock exercise, such as schizophrenia), and dispense antibiotics (Figure 9.2).[8]

According to a bioterrorism preparedness study released on December 14, 2004 by Trust for America's Health (an independent research group supported by The Robert Wood Johnson Foundation, the Bauman Foundation, and the New York Community Trust), only six states have "green" status with SNS, meaning only these jurisdictions are adequately prepared to distribute medicine and supplies in a bioterrorism emergency. Two-thirds of American states have scored six or less out of 10 possible indicators of overall readiness.[9]

Glossary

Abrasion—Injury from a scrape on the skin.

Abscess—A pocket of pus that accumulates in the body as a result of an infection.

Aerobic—Occurring in or requiring the presence of air.

Aerosolized organisms—Particles in the air that consist partially or wholly of microorganisms that have been expelled from the body, as during a sneeze or cough.

Agglutination test—A blood test designed to identify infectious microorganisms, in which lumping of microorganisms occurs after immune serum is added to a patient's blood culture.

Antibodies—Specialized proteins made by the immune system that bind to foreign organisms and protect the body against infectious diseases.

Antibiotic—A substance that kills or inhibits the growth of a microorganism.

Arthropod—A classification of animals that have jointed appendages and a segmented body, which includes insects, spiders, ticks, and mites.

Attenuated—Weakened.

Bacteremia—A bacterial infection that has entered the host's bloodstream.

Biogeography—The study of the distribution of plants, animals, and insects over land and water.

Bioterrorism—The use of bacteria, viruses, or the toxins produced by these microorganisms as weapons with the intention to disrupt or instill fear in society.

Bronchopneumonia—Inflammation of the bronchiole membranes of the lungs as a result of disease.

Case fatality rate—The proportion of cases of a disease that are fatal.

Contracted—To have acquired a condition.

Convalescence—The period of recovery after a disease or treatment.

Culture—Microorganisms grown in a laboratory for the purpose of analysis. Cultures usually require broth, agar, or gelatin as a growth nutrient medium. Blood cultures involve a sample of blood from a patient or an animal.

Deoxyribonucleic acid (DNA)—The chemical that contains all the genetic information of the cell.

100

Differential diagnosis—Diagnosis based on a comparison of symptoms between two or more similar diseases.

Ecological—Relating to the relationship between living organisms and their environment.

ELISA—A test used to detect antibodies in the blood; stands for enzyme-linked immunosorbant assay.

Endemic—A persistent presence of disease in a certain population.

Enzootic—Persistent presence of a disease in animals (with the implication that the disease may affect the human population in that geographic area).

Epidemiologist—A scientist who studies diseases or conditions in the human population and the factors that affect them.

Epidemiology—The study of patterns in, and factors influencing, diseases or conditions in human populations.

Etiology—The cause of a disease.

False positive—A positive test result for a patient who does not have the condition.

Gram-negative—A category of bacteria (such as *Francisella tularensis*) that do not retain the purple coloring during the Gram stain method.

Gram-positive—A category of bacteria that retain the crystal violet stain and purple coloring during the Gram stain method.

Host—An organism that is infected with or colonized by a microorganism.

Infectious—Capable of being passed from one organism to another through the transmission of disease-causing microorganisms.

Infiltrates—Fluid or substances deposited in and diffused through a tissue, organ, or cell.

Inflammation—A defensive reaction of the body in which tissues swell, redden, and become painful in the affected area; the condition is associated with the activity of immune system cells.

Intramuscular injection—The administration of a drug through a needle placed within a muscle.

Isolated cases—Incidences of a disease that occur infrequently and with no connection to other events.

Laboratory-acquired—A disease or condition that is attributed to an exposure resulting from work in a scientific or clinical occupational setting.

Glossary

Lesion—A skin wound.

Leukocytes—White blood cells.

Lymph node—Part of the lymphatic system that filters microorganisms from tissues and contains white blood cells that recognize and fight pathogens.

Lymphadenitis—Inflammation due to the drainage of bacteria into the lymph nodes that produces swelling, pain, and tenderness.

Lymphocyte—A type of white blood cell, a T cell or B cell.

Macrophage—A type of white blood cell that engulfs and kills microorganisms.

Meningitis—Inflammation of the membranes surrounding the spinal cord and brain.

Morbidity—A state of illness or sickness.

Mortality—The rate of death caused by a disease in a given population.

Needle aspiration—Removal of fluid from a body site through a thin small needle.

Notifiable disease—Disease or infectious disease agent that must be reported to a health department or government official.

Outbreak—A sudden rise in the number of cases of a disease in a given population.

Parasite—An organism that obtains nutrients or shelter from, and to the detriment of, another organism.

Pathogen—Disease-causing microorganism.

Polymerase chain reaction (PCR)—A method to copy DNA.

Phagocytosis—The process by which immune cells, such as macrophages, engulf and digest infectious agents or foreign substances.

Pleural effusion—Escape of fluid into the linings of the lungs.

Pneumonic—Relating to or affecting the lungs.

Primer—A small piece of DNA used in PCR to start the copying procedure.

Reservoir—A host that harbors a parasite or pathogen and allows it to perform significant aspects of its life cycle.

Resistance—The ability of a pathogen to resist and survive the effects of a drug or substance used against it.

Sentinel event—The first case of a rare or unexpected disease in an environment, which signals that a possible outbreak is about to unfold.

Sepsis—A poisoned state that results when disease-causing bacteria and toxins enter a patient's bloodstream.

Survival rate—The proportion of people affected with a disease who are alive after a given length of time has passed.

Tick-borne—Carried by a tick.

Transovarial transmission—Passage of a microorganism to succeeding generations of an arthropod (*e.g.*, from female to developing ova).

Transstadial transmission—Passage of a microorganism from one stage of the life cycle to another.

Transmission—Any mechanism by which an infectious agent is spread from one organism to another.

Ulcer—Lesion on the skin characterized by redness, swelling, and hardening around the affected area, as well as blistering, fluid weeping, and a loss of the upper layer of skin.

Vectors—Organisms such as flies, fleas, and ticks that carry and transmit pathogenic microorganisms to other organisms.

Virulence—The degree of disease-causing capability of a microorganism.

Waterborne—Transported in or transmitted through water, as of a pathogenic microorganism.

Zoonotic—Disease that can be transmitted from animals to humans.

Notes

CHAPTER 1

1 Pape, J., K. Gershman, J. Petersen, D. D. Ferguson, J. E. Staples. "Tularemia Associated with a Hamster Bite–Colorado, 2004." *MMWR* (53) (January 7, 2005): 1202.

CHAPTER 2

1 Wherry W. B., B. H. Lamb. "A New Bacterial Disease of Rodents Transmissible to Man." *Journal of Infectious Disease* 15(1914): 331.

2 Francis, E. "Deer-fly Fever or Pahvant Valley Plague: A Disease of Man of Hither-to-Unknown Etiology." *Public Health Reports* 36(September 12, 1919): 2061.

3 Francis, E. "Tularemia." *Public Health Reports* 36(1921): 1731–1738.

4 Francis, E. "A Summary of Present Knowledge of Tularemia." *Medicine* 7(1928): 411.

CHAPTER 3

1 de la Cruz, P., L. Cummings, D. Harmon, D. Mosier, P. Johannes, J. Lawler, F. Pintz, K. Senger, T. Dosch, and Division of Bacterial Diseases, Division of Vector-Borne Viral Diseases, Center for Infectious Diseases, CDC. "Outbreak of Tick-borne Tularemia—South Dakota" *MMWR* 33(42)(October 26, 1984): 601–602.

2 Taylor, J. P., G. R. Istre, T. C. McChesney, F. T. Satalowich, R. L. Parker, L. M. McFarland. "Epidemiologic Characteristics of Human Tularemia in the Southwest-Central States, 1981–1987." *American Journal of Epidemiology* 133(10): 1032–1038.

3 Anda, P., J. S. del Pozo, J. M. D. García, et al. "Waterborne Outbreak of Tularemia Associated with Crayfish Fishing." *Emerging Infectious Diseases* 7(3) Supplement (2001): 575–582.

CHAPTER 4

1 Francis, E. "Sources of Infection and Seasonal Incidence of Tularemia in Man." *Public Health Reports* 22 (1937): 103–113.

2 Tärnvik, A., L. Berglund. "Tularaemia." *European Respiratory Journal* 21(2003): 361–373.

CHAPTER 5

1. CIDRAP "Tularemia: Current, comprehensive information on pathogenesis, microbiology, epidemiology, diagnosis, treatment, and prophylaxis." http://www.cidrap.umn.edu/

2. Ericsson, M., G. Sandstrom, A. Sjostedt, A.Tarnvik. "Persistence of Cell-mediated Immunity and Decline of Humoral Immunity to the Intracellular Bacterium *Francisella tularensis* 25 Years after Natural Infection." *Journal of Infectious Diseases* 170(1994): 110–114.

3. Johansson, A., M. Forsman, A. Sjöstedt. "The Development of Tools for Diagnosis of Tularemia and Typing of *Franciella tularensis*." *Acta Pathologica Microbiologica et Immunological Scandinavica (APMIS)* 112(2004): 898–907.

CHAPTER 6

1. Parkin, W. E. "Tularemia–New Jersey." *MMWR* 35(48) (December 5, 1986): 747–748, 753.

2. Young, L. S., D. S. Bicknell, B. G Archer, et al. "Tularemia Epidemic: Vermont, 1968. Forty-seven Cases Linked to Contact with Muskrats." *N Engl J Med* 280(1969): 1253–1260.

3. Drummond, Roger. *Ticks and What You Can Do About Them.* Berkeley, CA: Wilderness Press, 1990.

CHAPTER 7

1 Smith, Stephen, Scott Allen. "Probe of Boston University Lab Illnesses Looks to a Lurking Contaminant." *Boston Globe* (January 5, 2005).

2 Feldman, K. A., R. E. Enscore, S. L. Lathrop, et al. "An Outbreak of Primary Pulmonary Tularemia on Martha's Vineyard." *New England Journal of Medicine* 345(22)(2001): 826–828.

3 Feldman, K. A., R. E. Enscore, S. L. Lathrop, et al. "An Outbreak of Primary Pulmonary Tularemia on Martha's Vineyard." *New England Journal of Medicine* 345(22)(2001): 1601–1606.

4 McCarthy, V. P., M. D. Murphy. "Lawnmower Tularemia." *Pediatric Infectious Disease Journal* 9(4)(1990): 298–300.

5 Burrell, Chris. "Landscapers to Be Tested for Tularemia." *Vineyard Gazette* (September 19, 2003).

6 Klemets, Peter, Markku Kuusi, Pekka Nuorti."Outbreak of tularaemia in Finland." *Eurosurveillance Weekly* 4(32)(2000).

7 Eliasson, H., J. Lindbäck, J. Pekka Nuorti, et al. "The 2000 Tularemia Outbreak: Study of Risk Factors in Disease-Endemic and Emergent Area, Sweden." *Emerging Infectious Diseases* 9(2002): 956–960.

8 Pomanskaia, L. A. "The Survival Times of the Organisms of Tularaemia on Grain and Straw." *Journal of Microbiology, Epidemiology and Immunology* 28(1957): 597–603.

CHAPTER 8

1 Harris, S. "Japanese Biological Warfare Research on Humans: A Case Study of Microbiology and Ethics." *Annals of The New York Academy of Sciences* 666(1992): 21–52.

2 Alibek, Ken. *BioHazard.* New York, NY: Dell Publishing, 1999.

3 O'Neal, Glenn. "Behind the Biowarfare 'Eight Ball.'" *USA Today* (December 20, 2001).

4 Torok, T. J., R. V. Tauxe, R. P. Wise, et al. "A Large Community Outbreak of Salmonellosis Caused by Intentional Contamination of Restaurant Salad Bars." *JAMA* 278(1997): 389–395.

5 Pavlin, J. A. "Epidemiology of Bioterrorism." *Emerging Infectious Diseases* 5(4)(July/August 1999): 528–530.

6 Treadwell, T. A., D. Koo, K. Kuker, A. S. Khan. "Epidemiologic Clues to Bioterrorism." *Public Health Reports* 118(March/April 2003): 92–98.

7 Dembek, Z. F., R. L. Buckman, S. K. Fowler, J. L. Hadler. "Missed Sentinel Case of Naturally Occurring Pneumonic Tularemia Outbreak: Lessons for Detection of Bioterrorism." *Journal of the American Board of Family Practitioners* 16(4)(July–August 2003) 339–342.

8 Kaufmann, A. F., M. I. Meltzer, G. P. Schmid. "The Economic Impact of a Bioterrorist Attack: Are Prevention and Postattack Intervention Programs Justifiable?" *Emerging Infectious Diseases* 3(1997): 83–94.

CHAPTER 9

1 Pollitzer, R. *Review of Russian Papers on Tularemia.* Bethesda, MD: 1958.

2 Saslaw, S., H. T. Eigelsbach, J. A. Prior, H. E. Wilson, S. Carhart. "Tularemia Vaccine Study. II. Respiratory challenge." *Archives of Internal Medicine* 107(1961): 702–714.

3 Burke, D. S. "Immunization against Tularemia: Analysis of the Effectiveness of Live *Francisella tularensis* Vaccine in Prevention of Laboratory-Acquired Tularemia." *Journal of Infectious Diseases* 135(1977): 55–60.

4 Lang, Leslie H. "NIH Awards $3.5 million grant to Frelinger for biodefense." University of North Carolina at Chapel Hill news release (558). November 12, 2004.

Notes

5   Dr. Inzana's research *http://www.vate-chalumni.com/chapters/index.html?speakers/inzana.htm*

6   Dr. Cooper's research *www.ecpe.vt.edu/news/ar04/photonic.html*

7   Altonn, Helen. "State Tests Response to Bioterror." *Honolulu Star-Bulletin* (May 20, 2004).

8   Majors, B. "Hundreds 'Sick' from Bacteria Exposure." *Oak Ridger* (August 6, 2004).

9   Trust for America. *Bioterrorism Preparedness Study*, December 14, 2004.

Bibliography

Alibek, Ken. *BioHazard*. New York, NY: Dell Publishing, 1999.

Altonn, Helen. "State Tests Response to Bioterror." *Honolulu Star-Bulletin* (May 20, 2004).

American Academy of Pediatrics Committee on Environmental Health. "Follow Safety Precautions When Using DEET on Children." *AAP News* (June 2003).

Anda, P., J. S. del Pozo, J. M. D. García, et al. "Waterborne Outbreak of Tularemia Associated with Crayfish Fishing." *Emerging Infectious Diseases* 7(3) Supplement (2001): 575–582.

Belding, D. L., B. Merrill. "Tularemia in Imported Rabbits in Massachusetts." *New England Journal of Medicine* 224(1941): 1085–1087.

Burke, D. S. "Immunization against Tularemia: Analysis of the Effectiveness of Live *Francisella tularensis* Vaccine in Prevention of Laboratory-Acquired Tularemia." *Journal of Infectious Diseases* 135(1977): 55–60.

Burrell, Chris. "Landscapers to Be Tested for Tularemia." *Vineyard Gazette* (September 19, 2003).

M. Chang, M. K. Glynn, Samuel L. Groseclose. "Endemic, Notifiable Bioterrorism-related Diseases, United States, 1992–1999." *Emerging Infectious Diseases* 9(5)(2003): 556–564.

Christopher, G. W., T. J. Cieslak, J. A. Pavlin, and E. M. Eitzen Jr. "Biological Warfare. A Historical Perspective." *JAMA* 278(5)(1997): 412–417.

de la Cruz, P., L. Cummings, D. Harmon, D. Mosier, P. Johannes, J. Lawler, F. Pintz, K. Senger, T. Dosch, and Division of Bacterial Diseases, Division of Vector-Borne Viral Diseases, Center for Infectious Diseases, CDC. "Outbreak of Tick-borne Tularemia—South Dakota" *MMWR* 33(42)(October 26, 1984): 601–602.

Dembek, Z. F., R. L. Buckman, S. K. Fowler, J. L. Hadler. "Missed Sentinel Case of Naturally Occurring Pneumonic Tularemia Outbreak: Lessons for Detection of Bioterrorism." *Journal of the American Board of Family Practitioners* 16(4)(July–August 2003) 339–342.

Dennis, D. T., T. V. Inglesby, D. A. Henderson, et al., for the Working Group on Civilian Biodefense. "Tularemia as a Biological Weapon." *JAMA* 285(21)(June 6, 2001): 2763–2773.

107

Bibliography

Drummond, Roger. *Ticks and What You Can Do About Them.* Berkeley, CA: Wilderness Press, 1990.

Eliasson, H., J. Lindbäck, J. Pekka Nuorti, et al. "The 2000 Tularemia Outbreak: Study of Risk Factors in Disease-Endemic and Emergent Area, Sweden." *Emerging Infectious Diseases* 9(2002): 956–960.

Ericsson, M., G. Sandstrom, A. Sjostedt, A.Tarnvik. "Persistence of Cell-mediated Immunity and Decline of Humoral Immunity to the Intracellular Bacterium *Francisella tularensis* 25 Years after Natural Infection." *Journal of Infectious Diseases* 170(1994): 110–114.

Evans, M. E., D. W. Gregory, W. Schaffner, Z. A. McGee. "Tularemia: A 30-Year Experience With 88 Cases." *Medicine* 64(4)(1985): 251–269.

Evans, M. E., A. M. Friedlander. "Tularemia," *Textbook of Military Medicine: Medical Aspects of Chemical and Biological Warfare.* Washington, DC: U.S. Dept. of the Army, The Surgeon General, and the Borden Institute, 1997, pp. 503–512.

Feldman, K. A., R. E. Enscore, S. L. Lathrop, et al. "An Outbreak of Primary Pulmonary Tularemia on Martha's Vineyard." *New England Journal of Medicine* 345(22)(2001): 1601–1606.

Feldman, K. A. "Tularemia." *Journal of the American Veterinary Medical Association* 222(6)(2003): 725–730.

Feldman, K. A., D. Stiles-Enos, K. Julian, et al. "Tularemia on Martha's Vineyard: Seroprevalence and Occupational Risk." *Emerging Infectious Diseases* 9(3)(2003): 350–354.

Francis, E. "The Occurrence of Tularemia in Nature as a Disease of Man." *Public Health Reports* 36 (1921): 1731–1738.

Francis, E. "A Summary of Present Knowledge of Tularemia." *Medicine* 7(1928): 411–432.

Francis, E. "Sources of Infection and Seasonal Incidence of Tularemia in Man." *Public Health Reports* 22 (1937): 103–113.

Harris, S. "Japanese Biological Warfare Research on Humans: A Case Study of Microbiology and Ethics." *Annals of The New York Academy of Sciences* 666(1992): 21–52.

Hornick, R. "Tularemia Revisited." *New England Journal of Medicine* 345(2001): 1637–1639.

Jellison, W. L. "Tularemia." *Bulletins on the History of Medicine* 96(1972): 477–485.

Johansson, A., M. Forsman, A. Sjöstedt. "The Development of Tools for Diagnosis of Tularemia and Typing of *Franciella tularensis*." *Acta Pathologica Microbiologica et Immunological Scandinavica (APMIS)* 112(2004): 898–907.

Kaufmann, A. F., M. I. Meltzer, G. P. Schmid. "The Economic Impact of a Bioterrorist Attack: Are Prevention and Postattack Intervention Programs Justifiable?" *Emerging Infectious Diseases* 3(1997): 83–94.

Klemets, Peter, Markku Kuusi, Pekka Nuorti. "Outbreak of Tularaemia in Finland." *Eurosurveillance Weekly* 4(32)(2000).

Klock, L. E., P. F. Olsen, T. Fukushima. "Tularemia Epidemic Associated with the Deerfly." *JAMA* 226(2)(1973): 149–152.

Lang, Leslie H. "NIH Awards $3.5 Million Grant to Frelinger for Biodefense." University of North Carolina at Chapel Hill news release (558). November 12, 2004.

Lilienfeld, David E., Paul D. Stolley. *Foundations of Epidemiology*, Third Edition. New York, NY: Oxford University Press, 1994.

Majors, B. "Hundreds 'Sick' from Bacteria Exposure." *Oak Ridger* (August 6, 2004).

McCarthy, V. P., M. D. Murphy. "Lawnmower Tularemia." *Pediatric Infectious Disease Journal* 9(4)(1990): 298–300.

Hayes, E., S. Marshall, D. Dennis, K. Feldman. "Tularemia–United States, 1990–2000." *MMWR* 51(09)(2002): 182–184.

New York City Department of Health and Mental Hygiene. *Medical Treatment and Response to Suspected Tularemia: Information for Health Care Providers During Biologic Emergencies.* July 2000 (draft).

Nolte, K. B., R. L. Hanzlick, D. C. Payne, et al. "Medical Examiners, Coroners, and Bioterrorism: A Guidebook for Surveillance and Case Management." *MMWR* 53(RR-8)(2004): 1–27.

O'Neal, Glenn. "Behind the Biowarfare 'Eight Ball.'" *USA Today* (December 20, 2001).

Pape, J., K. Gershman, J. Petersen, D. D. Ferguson, J. E. Staples. "Tularemia Associated with a Hamster Bite–Colorado, 2004." *MMWR* 53 (January 7, 2005): 1202.

Parkin, W. E. "Tularemia–New Jersey." *MMWR* 35(48) (December 5, 1986): 747–748, 753.

Bibliography

Parola, P., D. Raoult. "Ticks." *Clinical Infectious Diseases* 32(2001): 897–928.

Pavlin, J. A. "Epidemiology of Bioterrorism." *Emerging Infectious Diseases* 5(4)(July/August 1999): 528–530.

Perez-Castrillon, J. L., P. Bachiller-Luque, M. Martin-Luquero, et al. "Tularemia Epidemic in Northwestern Spain: Clinical Description and Therapeutic Response." *Clinical Infectious Diseases* 33(4)(2001): 573–576.

Pollitzer, R. *Review of Russian Papers on Tularemia.* Bethesda, MD: 1958.

Pollitzer, R. *History and Incidence of Tularemia in the Soviet Union: A Review.* New York, NY: Institute of Contemporary Russian Studies, Fordham University, 1967.

Pomanskaia, L. A. "The Survival Times of the Organisms of Tularaemia on Grain and Straw." *Journal of Microbiology, Epidemiology and Immunology* 28(1957): 597–603.

Rohrbach, B. W., E. Westerman, G. R. Istre. "Epidemiology and Clinical Characteristics of Tularemia in Oklahoma, 1979–1985." *Southern Medical Journal* 84(9)(1991): 1091–1096.

Rotz, L., A. S. Khan, S. R. Lillibridge, S. M. Ostroff, J. M. Hughes. "Public Health Assessment of Potential Biological Terrorism Agents." *Emerging Infectious Diseases* 8(2)(February 2002): 225–230.

Saslaw, S., H. T. Eigelsbach, J. A. Prior, H. E. Wilson, S. Carhart. "Tularemia Vaccine Study. II. Respiratory Challenge." *Archives of Internal Medicine* 107(1961): 702–714.

Simpson, Walter M. *Tularemia: History, Pathology, Diagnosis and Treatment.* New York, NY: Paul B. Hoeber, 1929.

Smith, Stephen, Scott Allen. "Probe of Boston University Lab Illnesses Looks to a Lurking Contaminant." *Boston Globe* (January 5, 2005).

Sjostedt, A., U. Eriksson, L. Berglund, A. Tarnvik. "Detection of *Francisella tularensis* in Ulcers of Patients with Tularemia by PCR." *Journal of Clinical Microbiology* 35(1997): 1045–1048.

Syrjala, H., P. Kujala, V. Myllyla, A. Salminen. "Airborne Transmission of Tularemia in Farmers." *Scandinavian Journal of Infectious Diseases* 17(1985): 371–375.

Tärnvik, A., L. Berglund. "Tularaemia." *European Respiratory Journal* 21(2003): 361–373.

Taylor, J. P., G. R. Istre, T. C. McChesney, et al. "Epidemiologic Characteristics of Human Tularemia in the Southwest-Central States, 1981–1987." *American Journal of Epidemiology* 133(10): 1032–1038.

Thorpe, B. B., et al. "Tularemia in Wildlife and Livestock of the Great Salt Lake Desert Region, 1951–1964." *American Journal of Tropical Medicine and Hygiene* 14(1965): 622–637.

Timmreck, Thomas C. *An Introduction to Epidemiology.* Boston, MA: Jones and Bartlett Publishers, 1994.

Torok, T. J., R. V. Tauxe, R. P. Wise, et al. "A Large Community Outbreak of Salmonellosis Caused by Intentional Contamination of Restaurant Salad Bars." *JAMA* 278(1997): 389–395.

Treadwell, T. A., D. Koo, K. Kuker, A. S. Khan. "Epidemiologic Clues to Bioterrorism." *Public Health Reports* 118(March/April 2003): 92–98.

Trust for America. *Bioterrorism Preparedness Study,* December 14, 2004.

Williams, J., G. Tallis, C. Dalton, S. Ng, S. Beaton, M. Catton, J. Elliott, J. Carnie. "Community Outbreak of Psittacosis in a Rural Australian Town." *Lancet* 351(1998): 1697–1699.

World Health Organization meeting in Bath, UK, September 14–15, 2003. "Improving Public Health Preparedness for and Response to the Threat of Epidemics: Tularemia Network."

Young L. S., D. S. Bicknell, B. G Archer, et al. "Tularemia Epidemic: Vermont, 1968. Forty-seven Cases Linked to Contact with Muskrats." *N Engl J Med* 280(1969): 1253–1260.

Further Reading

Benenson, Abram S. *Control of Communicable Diseases Manual.* Sixteenth Edition. Washington: American Public Health Association, 1995.

McInnes, Mary Elizabeth. *Essentials of Communicable Disease.* Second Edition. St. Louis: The C.V. Mosby Company, 1975.

Wong, J. D., Shapiro, D. S. "Francisella." In: Murray P. R., Baron E. J., Pfaller M. A., et al., eds. *Manual of Clinical Microbiology.* Seventh Edition. Washington, D.C.: American Society for Microbiology Press, 1999: 647–651.

Websites

Biological Weapons
http://news.nationalgeographic.com/news/
2001/10/1012_wirebioweapons2.html

Bioterrorism Agents—Tularemia
Centers for Disease Control and Prevention (CDC)
http://www.bt.cdc.gov/agent/agentlist.asp

CDC National Center for Health Statistics
http://www.cdc.gov/nchs/Default.htm

Center for Infectious Disease Research and Policy, University of Minnesota.
CIDRAP "Tularemia: Current, comprehensive information on pathogenesis, microbiology, epidemiology, diagnosis, treatment, and prophylaxis."
http://www.cidrap.umn.edu/cidrap/content/bt/tularemia/index.html

Department of Health and Human Services, United States Government.
Civilian Preparedness for Biological Warfare and Terrorism:
HHS Readiness and Role in Vaccine Research and Development.
Tommy G. Thompson, Secretary, U.S. Department of Health
and Human Services, Tuesday, October 23, 2001
http://www.hhs.gov/asl/testify/t011023.html

Dr. Cooper's Research on Tularemia Biosensor
http://www.ecpe.vt.edu/news/ar04/photonic.html

Dr. Inzana's Research
http://www.research.vt.edu/resmag/2002summer/rapid.html

National Institutes of Health (NIH)
http://www.nih.gov/

Report on Public Health Preparedness, Trust for America's Health
http://healthyamericans.org/reports/bioterror04/

U.S. Army Medical Research Institute of
Infectious Diseases (USAMRIID)
http://www.dcmilitary.com/army/standard/10_05/
local_news/33582-1.html

Websites

U.S. Public Health Service (PHS)
http://www.usphs.gov/html/agencies_programs.html

U.S. Strategic National Stockpile (SNS)
http://www.bt.cdc.gov/stockpile/

Index

Agglutination test
development, 18, 25
and tularemia, 18,
25, 36, 51–54, 60
Alibek, Dr. Ken, 81–83
Anthrax, 50, 69
as biological weapon,
6, 47, 81, 86,
90–91, 93, 97
Antibiotics
treatment of disease,
7–8, 37, 40, 45, 54,
58–59, 77, 81, 84,
96–98
Antibodies, 18, 94–95
testing, 49, 51–54,
60–61, 68, 73, 76
Antigens, 18, 94

*Bacillus tularense. See
Francisella tularensis*
Bacteria, 55
and diseases, 8–9, 12,
17, 21, 23, 26–27,
31, 36, 39, 43, 45,
49–53, 61, 63, 66,
69, 72, 81, 94–95
gram-negative,
37–39, 59
gram-positive, 37
Bacteremia
causes, 36–37
Biological warfare
categories, 46–47, 86
costs of, 90
Francisella tularensis,
13, 15, 44, 47,
79–90
impact of, 89–90
research, 79–83, 94
responses and pre-
vention, 87–90,
95, 98

terrorism, 84–86, 88,
91, 96–97, 99
types, 6, 46–47,
79–81, 86, 91
Biopreparat, 15, 81–82
Botulism, 47, 86
Bronchopneumonia, 37,
88
Brucellosis, 13, 25, 47,
50, 90

CDC. *See* Centers for
Disease Control and
Prevention
Centers for Disease
Control and Preven-
tion (CDC), 49
laboratory response
network, 60, 68,
70–71
pharmaceutical
stockpile, 96
and public health,
33, 46, 89–90
Chapin, Dr. Charles C.,
17–18, 20, 25
Cholera, 6, 32, 47
Conjunctivitis tularensis,
14, 20
Cooper, Dr. Kristie, 94
Cryptosporidiosis, 6, 47

DDT, 6
Deerfly
outbreaks, 14, 17,
19–24, 27–29, 33
DEET
invention of, 64–66
Deoxyribonucleic acid
(DNA)
testing of, 8, 54–57
DFA. *See* Direct fluorescent antibody stain

Diagnosis, tularemia,
37, 42
agglutination test,
18, 25, 36, 51–54,
60
antibody tests, 49,
51–54, 60–61, 68,
76
cultures, 8, 31, 36, 39,
49, 51–54, 78, 89
DFA, 51
differential, 48–50
ELISA, 52–54
PCR, 8, 54–57
Diphtheria, 6, 50, 80
Direct fluorescent
antibody stain
(DFA), 51
DNA. *See* Deoxyribo-
nucleic acid

Ebola virus, 93
"Eight ball," 82–85
ELISA. *See* Enzyme-
linked immuno-
sorbant assay
Enzyme-linked
immunosorbant
assay (ELISA), 52–54
Epidemiology
observational, 33,
74–75
of tularemia, 9–12,
14–15, 21–22,
26–35, 51–54, 61,
72–73, 76–77

Feldman, Dr. Katherine,
73, 75–76
Francis, Dr. Edward
diseases of, 23
research of, 17, 19,
21–25, 32

115

Index

Picture Credits

9: © Ted Horowitz/Corbis
18: © Peter Lamb, HFS Imaging
19: © Rick Poley/Visuals Unlimited
23: National Library of Medicine
29: Public Health Image Library (PHIL), CDC
34: Morbidity and Mortality Weekly Report (MMWR)
38: © Jack Bostrack/Visuals Unlimited
39: Public Health Image Library (PHIL), CDC
41: Public Health Image Library (PHIL), CDC
43: © Peter Lamb, HFS Imaging
44: Emerging Infectious Diseases (EID)
45: © Peter Lamb, HFS Imaging
51: Public Health Image Library (PHIL), CDC

53: © Peter Lamb, HFS Imaging
57: © Peter Lamb, HFS Imaging
59: © Peter Lamb, HFS Imaging
62: LLC/FogStock/IndexOpen
65: © Peter Lamb, HFS Imaging
66: University of Nebraska Department of Entomology
70: © Peter Lamb, HFS Imaging
71: CDC/PHIL/Corbis
83: Associated Press, AP
83: Associated Press, U.S. Army
83: Associated Press, AP
83: Associated Press, AP

Cover: © Peter Lamb, HFS Imaging

About the Author

Susan Hutton Siderovski began her career as a Certified Public Health Inspector and obtained a Bachelor's of Applied Science degree in Environmental Health from Ryerson University in 1987. Mrs. Siderovski worked as a certified inspector in the following Ontario cities: Belleville, Trenton, Kingston, Sharbot Lake, and Whitby. Given her interest in infectious disease, she attended Queen's University in Kingston, Ontario and recieved a Master of Science degree in Community Health and Epidemiology in 1989.

Mrs. Siderovski's research into indoor air quality, blue-green algal blooms in recreational waters, cancer cluster investigation methods, and health outcome evaluations have led to published articles in the *Environmental Health Review, Canadian Journal of Public Health*, and the *Journal of the Canadian Evaluation Society*. She has made presentations at the Ontario Public Health Association, Ontario Branch (Canadian Institute of Public Health Inspectors), and Association of Ontario Public Health Epidemiologists scientific meetings.

Mrs. Siderovski's career in public health epidemiology led to a return to her alma mater to teach Epidemiology and Health Administration at Ryerson University. Her recent relocation to the United States with her husband (Dr. David P. Siderovski, Associate Professor of Pharmacology, University of North Carolina–Chapel Hill) has provided opportunities for her to do scientific writing, assist in laboratory work, volunteer in the Chapel Hill–Carrboro City Schools, and devote time to raising their two children, Peter and Karen.

About the Founding Editor

The late I. Edward Alcamo was a Distinguished Teaching Professor of Microbiology at the State University of New York at Farmingdale. Alcamo studied biology at Iona College in New York and earned his M.S. and Ph.D. degrees in microbiology at St. John's University, also in New York. He had taught at Farmingdale for over 30 years. In 2000, Alcamo won the Carski Award for Distinguished Teaching in Microbiology, the highest honor for microbiology teachers in the United States. He was a member of the American Society for Microbiology, the National Association of Biology Teachers, and the American Medical Writers Association. Alcamo authored numerous books on the subjects of microbiology, AIDS, and DNA technology as well as the award-winning textbook *Fundamentals of Microbiology*, now in its sixth edition.